"The world doesn't deserve Betty White, but thankfully, she shares her wisdom, humor, and compassion with us all. Paula Bernstein's joyful book brims with priceless life lessons from an unconventional woman who blazed trails while marching to her own beat. Indeed, we should all ask ourselves: *What would Betty do?*"

—ERIN CARLSON,
author of *Queen Meryl* and *I'll Have What She's Having*

* * *

"This book makes it clear Betty White's pioneering ways in the world of television and in the characters she plays are no joke—her humor, resilience, and refusal to live up to tired stereotypes at all stages of her career prove her to be an inspirational role model for all of us."

—LAUREN MARINO,
author of *What Would Dolly Do?* and *Bookish Broads*

* * *

"It's obvious that we could all learn a thing or ten from the incredible Betty White. Thankfully, the funny and delightful Paula Bernstein has compiled a whole book of gorgeous lessons gleaned from the life of this spectacular talent."

—SARA BENINCASA,
author of *Real Artists Have Day Jobs* and *Agorafabulous!*

* * *

"I had no idea that the same woman who often played sweet, naive characters on TV was actually a brave feminist trailblazer in real life. This fun book captures Betty's positive outlook on life and explains the reason she continues to be such an icon."

—MELISSA MAERZ,
author of *Alright, Alright, Alright: The Oral History of Richard Linklater's Dazed and Confused*

"Everyone loves Betty White and after reading Paula Bernstein's *How to Be Golden*, it'd be impossible not to absolutely idolize the sitcom star. Bernstein's tome is a lovely and sweet blend of biography and advice where Betty's voice is loud and clear. One of the quintessential stars of any age shines through in a loving story you'll want to return to as you navigate life. A definite golden joy on its own!"

—KRISTEN LOPEZ,
IndieWire TV Editor

* * *

"What a fun tribute to an American icon! Paula's book is insightful and funny, just like the incomparable Betty White herself!"

—ALEXI PAPPAS,
Olympic runner and author of *Bravey*

* * *

"Paula Bernstein's *How to Be Golden* isn't simply a biography of film and television icon Betty White; full of surprising trivia, fun quizzes, behind the scenes stories and more, it's a tribute to one of Hollywood's most beloved and resilient comedians of all time."

—ERIK ANDERSON,
AwardsWatch

* * *

"With *How to Be Golden*, Paula Bernstein has crafted the perfect tribute to an American icon. In a format that parses through the entire century of Betty's life and career, this lively book informs us about her incredible past and provides life lessons that we, too, can use to Betty-er ourselves."

—JIM COLUCCI,
author of *Golden Girls Forever: An Unauthorized Look Behind the Lanai*

HOW TO BE GOLDEN

Lessons We Can Learn from Betty White

PAULA BERNSTEIN

RUNNING PRESS

PHILADELPHIA

Running Press
Hachette Book Group
1290 Avenue of the Americas, New York, NY 10104
www.runningpress.com
@Running_Press

Printed in the United States of America

First Edition: October 2021

Published by Running Press, an imprint of Perseus Books, LLC, a subsidiary of
Hachette Book Group, Inc. The Running Press name and logo is a trademark
of the Hachette Book Group.

The Hachette Speakers Bureau provides a wide range of authors for speaking events.
To find out more, go to www.hachettespeakersbureau.com or call (866) 376-6591.

Cover and interior illustrations by Louisa Cannell.
Print book cover and interior design by Marissa Raybuck.

Library of Congress Control Number: 2021935412

ISBNs: 978-0-7624-7459-2 (hardcover), 978-0-7624-7460-8 (ebook)

LSC-C

Printing 1, 2021

To Jess and Ruby,
for making my life so much brighter.

Contents

INTRODUCTION

As a child growing up in the 1970s and 1980s, it felt as if Betty White was everywhere. Given how much TV I watched, she sort of was! Like a fairy godmother of TV, she brightened up every show she appeared on. She quipped with the best of them on *Hollywood Squares*, performed a song-and-dance routine on *The Love Boat*, and embodied the lovably naive Rose Nylund on *The Golden Girls*.

Though her characters' suggestive innuendos frequently flew over my head, Betty's underlying humor and kindness shined through. Back then, I had no real sense of her age, but that's because even then, she was ageless (or perhaps timeless). She typified what it meant to be grown-up—if one just happened to have a sparkling personality, a plucky attitude, and a job that involved making people laugh. Whether she was dressed in leather as a sexy biker chick in a skit on *The Carol Burnett*

Show or throwing a tantrum about her "poor soufflé" as "The Happy Homemaker" on *The Mary Tyler Moore Show*, the radiant Betty seemed to be having the time of her life. I didn't realize that by the time I had "discovered her," Betty White was already a show-business veteran, having broken into radio and "experimental" TV decades earlier. Like a lot of people who love Betty, I can measure my life through her career.

The Golden Girls showed up in prime time during my high school years, and I watched with my mother on the comfy leather couch in the cozy wood-paneled den of our suburban home. I appreciated the sassy humor of the "girls," but they seemed impossibly old at the time. As I edge closer to their demographic, I find them increasingly relatable!

My fifteen-year-old daughter, Ruby, is now the same age I was when I watched *The Golden Girls* with my mom, and she has a totally different connection with the fabulous Ms. White. Until I recently introduced her to *The Mary Tyler Moore Show* and *The Golden Girls*, Ruby primarily knew Betty from her "crotchety old lady" cameos on sitcoms like *Community* and *30 Rock* and from animated films like *Dr. Seuss' The Lorax* and *Toy Story 4*. That's the thing about Betty White—her appeal is timeless and we each feel a different connection with her.

This book doesn't pretend to be a biography of Betty White, nor did I have the honor of interviewing her. I don't profess to know what Betty White truly thinks and feels about the world. But after reading all of the books she's written as well as nearly everything that's ever been written about her and watching every interview with her and most of her performances, I have a good sense of her outlook on life. I made every effort to be faithful to the spirit of a modern American heroine known for her compassion, zest for life, work ethic, and integrity. With *How to Be Golden*, I hope to celebrate the amazing legacy she's created—and maybe even inspire others to live their most golden life!

CHAPTER ONE

GOLDEN BEGINNINGS

BETTY IS THE GRAND DAME OF SITCOMS, the first lady of television, a constant reassuring and entertaining presence in our living rooms and now on our phones and tablets. The technology may change, but Betty will always be on it, smiling naughtily—and making us smile with her—in reruns, which span generations. Why do we love Betty White so much? She's a role model, and not just because of her amazing work ethic and record-breaking career longevity. It's her outlook on life and love, her positive attitude, her openness to those who are different, and her passion for everything she does. A national treasure, Betty is one of the only things everyone can agree on.

Today when we picture Betty White, we think of her "wink and a nod" humor, her envelope-pushing performance on *Saturday Night Live* (*SNL*), and her iconic, Emmy Award–winning roles in some of the best TV sitcoms of all time. Of course, before she embodied Sue Ann Nivens, Rose Nylund, Elka Ostrovsky, or any of the other zany characters we remember her for, Betty White was just a little girl with big dreams—and big appetites! Her childhood was as sweet as a homemade brownie and as idyllic as a picture postcard, filled with family camping trips, lots of furry friends, and school plays— where, of course, she always landed the starring role. Even early on, the spotlight favored her. In fact, her youth could hardly have been more golden—and that's saying a lot, given she grew up during the Depression!

"Not Elizabeth . . . Betty"

Born on January 17, 1922, in Oak Park, Illinois, a suburb of Chicago, she was christened Betty Marion White. "Not Elizabeth . . . Betty. They didn't want any of the derivatives to sneak in . . . Liz, Lizzie, Liza, Beth. So, to leave no room for doubt, it was Betty," she later explained. Still, her mother managed to come up with a shorter nickname: "Bets."

Baby Betty moved with her family to Los Angeles before she turned two. In later years, she'd often joke that they moved to California before it gained statehood. (Not quite. That was back in 1850!) Still, Los Angeles looked quite different when her family settled on Sunset Boulevard. Back then, there was a stoplight at the end of the road rather than US Route 101. "Los Angeles has changed completely," she told Cynthia Littleton's *Variety* in 2020. "But when you see it through memory's eyes, you're not as conscious of those changes. You still see it the way you knew it."

When White's family arrived in Los Angeles, what we now know as the legendary Hollywood Sign in the Hollywood Hills had just been erected. Back then, it was *Hollywoodland*, meant to advertise a housing development (the *land* was removed when the sign was partially restored in 1949). It's not a stretch to say she grew up along with Hollywood, since when her family arrived in town, the golden age of Hollywood was just beginning. Movies were silent, TV didn't exist yet, and the first Academy Awards ceremony was still a few years away. Douglas Fairbanks Sr. and Mary Pickford were America's favorite movie star couple; other stars of the day included Greta Garbo, Louise Brooks, Joan Crawford, and Charlie Chaplin. Fertile soil for a young star-to-be!

But Betty's best childhood memories have little to do with Hollywood's glitz and glamour. As the beloved only child of Horace, an electrical engineer and traveling salesman, and Christine "Tess" White, a brunette homemaker with a broad smile, White said she was "spoiled rotten, but taught to appreciate it." Her grandparents were of Danish, Greek, English, and Welsh heritage. She inherited her optimism from her mother, who, by all accounts, could find the upside to just about any situation (again, it was the Depression!). "She always made the point that if you look at those negatives, you spoil all the good stuff and it goes by and you haven't tasted it," White later remembered.

As a salesman for an electrical company that produced floodlights for ballparks and sports stadiums, Horace was on the road a lot. Jovial and balding with dimples he passed on to his only child, Horace was hard-working, inventive, and bounding with energy. "Never satisfied with doing just two things at once if he could possibly squeeze in a third," Betty recalled. Her mother even dubbed him "Hurry Horace, the Hummingbird." In addition to the dimples, Betty clearly inherited Horace's need to constantly be working on something.

Horace and Tess had a bawdy sense of humor, and they didn't shy away from sharing jokes in front of their clever daughter. Her father would often repeat zingers he heard on the road—not all of them appropriate for children! "Dad would come home with these jokes, and he'd never explain them to me—if I caught on, fine, and if I didn't, that was fine," she recalled. Occasionally, he'd warn her: "I wouldn't take that one to school."

It was during mealtimes with her parents that she developed her quick wit and precise comic timing. She quickly learned that humor relies on timing. If you mess up the timing of the punch line, it kills the joke. That knack for comic timing served her well throughout her career. The only rule her family had about jokes? They had to be funny.

> ❝ If it was a little raunchy in the bargain, it had better be really funny enough to justify it. Merely dirty jokes didn't qualify.

LIFE LESSON:

Dream Big

As a child, when Betty dreamed of her future, she was a writer. Her favorite author was L. Frank Baum. It was originally her love of writing and reading that led her down the showbiz path. She and her parents devoured the Oz series, especially *The Wonderful Wizard of Oz* (which was adapted into the movie while Betty was in high school). The Oz series inspired her to experiment with screenwriting—at the age of eight! She wrote a short screenplay called "Trouble in Paradoz" with hopes she could cast Mae West (again, dream big!). By the age of eleven, she tried her hand at a novel she called "Cowgirl or Society." It was a rip-roaring western tale involving hunky cowboys, horse thieves, and a dog named Rusty. Her vivid imagination served her well at Horace Mann Grammar School in Los Angeles, where she wrote the graduation play, called "Land of the Rising Sun." "As any red-blooded American girl would do, I wrote myself in as the lead. I realized how much fun it was to be up on the stage. That was my first brush with anything in show business," she later said.

> 66
>
> **It was then that I contracted showbiz fever, for which there is no known cure.**

Long before future stars such as Carrie Fisher, Jamie Lee Curtis, Nicolas Cage, Angelina Jolie, Lenny Kravitz, and so many other future A-listers graduated from Beverly Hills High School, Betty White made her mark there. For her senior play, she starred as Elizabeth, the eldest and wisest of the Bennet sisters in Jane Austen's *Pride and Prejudice*. "We figured Jane Austen would have taken a dim view if we'd call the character Betty," she joked later.

Though her father initially wanted her to head to college after high school, Betty was eager to discover the world—and, more importantly, for the world to discover her! Inspired by her screen idol, the singer and actress Jeanette MacDonald (a huge star of the 1930s), she decided to pursue a career as an entertainer. Along with MacDonald's regular screen partner Nelson Eddy, "they were as important in my world, almost as important as my mother." You might think Betty's homemaker mother would have minded her daughter's interest in the limelight, but the senior Ms. White was an enlightened woman.

At a time when women were largely expected to marry young and start a family, it was bold of Betty to put her career ahead of home-making and child-rearing. Fortunately, her parents were thrilled with their little girl, no matter what she did. As long as it was big. Three months after her high school graduation in 1939, Betty got her first big break when she and the Beverly Hills High School student body president, Harry Bennett, sang and danced songs from *The Merry Widow* operetta on an experimental television show, the first of its kind on the West Coast.

The young brunette (she hadn't yet gone blonde!) decided to wear the nicest thing she owned, the dress she had just worn for high school graduation, a "fluffy white tulle number held up by a sapphire blue velvet ribbon halter." Filming in a makeshift studio on the fifth floor of the Packard Automobile building in downtown Los Angeles, the production was experimental. Betty remembered later that she and Harry had their faces covered with brown lipstick and white face paint to appear on black-and-white television (this was before color TV was invented!). Television was still such a new medium that nobody knew how to light actors properly, but it was clear that conventional "street" makeup wouldn't work.

To see their daughter on TV, Betty's parents had to crowd around the display cars in the building's first-floor Packard showroom to get a peek at the tiny monitor because they didn't have a TV at home. Then again, back then, almost nobody did. This experimental TV broadcast happened several months before RCA introduced television to Americans at the 1939 New York World's Fair in Queens. By 1940, only about ten thousand homes had a television. The first national broadcast didn't occur until 1951, by which time twelve million households had a television.

> **I was there when television first started. We grew up together.**

BETTY WHITE TRIVIA: World War II broke out just a month before Betty's twentieth birthday. Like many other performers (including Joan Crawford and Hattie McDaniel), she was happy to pitch in on the country's war effort. "At that point, you forgot all about show business, you forgot about everything except doing what you could do" to support the troops, she said later. As a member of the American Women's Voluntary Services (AWVS), Betty donned a uniform and drove a supply truck to soldiers who were temporarily housed in barracks in the Hollywood Hills and Santa Monica. She had only just gotten her driver's license! Then, at night, she'd lose the uniform and get gussied up for rec hall dances where Betty "would dance or play games or simply talk with the young men who were so far from home" before they were shipped overseas.

Pay to Play?

Believe it or not, Betty actually had to shell out money for her first "professional" experience. Operated by two character actors, the Bliss-Hayden Little Theatre, near Beverly Hills, wasn't an acting school *per se*, but it was a sure-fire way to gain experience. Betty "enrolled" and paid fifty dollars a month (a lot of money back then!) for the chance to try out for their monthly play. Guess who landed the lead in their next production? She realized then that acting "was just what I needed, and I realized that this is what I must do for the rest of my life."

When it came time to cast the next month's play, the theater directors shared some good news with Betty: not only would she be cast as the star, she wouldn't have to pay to play, so to speak. "It all seemed too good to be true. I was going to be able to stay around these nice people for another month; I had the lead in a marvelous play; best of all, I was going to get to work for *free!*" Just as Betty's mom could find a silver lining to every cloud, Betty was grateful for every opportunity—even if she had to make them happen for herself!

Create Your Own Opportunities

Betty made the rounds to the movie studios, hoping to launch a career in the style of her screen idol Jeanette MacDonald; but despite her classically beautiful heart-shaped face, hourglass figure, and warm smile, the gatekeepers decided she was not "photogenic" enough to be in pictures. At that particular moment, her farm-fed midwestern looks were out of fashion in Hollywood, which was enraptured by brooding beauties such as Greta Garbo, Marlene Dietrich, and Luise Rainer. Still, how could they not recognize the inner light and the outer beauty of young Betty?!

This was the point in her career at which many other young hopefuls packed their bags and went back home. Of course, in her case, home was Hollywood, so she didn't have far to go. Instead of giving up on her passion for acting, Betty decided to look beyond movies. It was still the golden age of radio, and if she didn't have a face for movies, she sure had a face for radio and a voice—and a personality—that sparkled.

> **You just keep plugging away. You don't give up.**

Fueled by her innate self-confidence, as well as her parents' unconditional support, Betty didn't wait around for promising opportunities to fall into her lap; she actively sought them out. That's how she ended up in the Taft Building, on the famed corner of Hollywood and Vine, with the ad agency that produced the popular radio show *The Great Gildersleeve*. She knew that Tuesday was casting day, so she hung around the office on Tuesdays. "I figured if they saw me often enough, they'd think they had hired me and then they'd give me another job," Betty said. "So I'd go there and I'd sit there and they'd say 'no, nothing today.'"

What do you know?! Her clever plan worked! One of the producers finally took pity on her and explained her predicament: she couldn't get a job unless she was a member of the radio performers' union (AFRA), and she couldn't become a member unless she got a job. The proverbial catch-22. How do you get past this? There is no answer to this riddle of a question, yet the sublime Ms. White cracked the nut. After what we assume was some dogged persistence, the producer at last agreed to give our aspiring thespian one word on a commercial on the radio show

The Great Gildersleeve so she could earn her union card. That one word? Parkay. The margarine brand, one of the show's sponsors, had only just been introduced (like Betty White, it continues to be popular).

That one word earned her a union card, which cost her sixty-seven dollars, which was thirty dollars more than the thirty-seven dollars she was paid for the gig. Short on cash, she had to borrow the rest of the money from her father. Thrilled that she got a job, Betty's father told her, "If you don't work too often, we can almost afford it." It was a good investment because with a union card in hand and some experience behind her, the newest union member was suddenly getting regular work. She continued to show up to radio castings, and she quickly learned that any time she was asked if she could do something, she should say YES even if she couldn't.

> 66
>
> **You said 'yes' to everything. Can you juggle? Sure.**

By exuding confidence beyond her years and bluffing about her experience, she was cast on a number of other popular radio shows at the time, including *Blondie,* based on the comic strip of the same name, and *This Is Your FBI,* the crime broadcast endorsed by none other than FBI director J. Edgar Hoover. She actually landed a spot on *This Is Your FBI* because another actress named Betty White didn't show up to the interview and there was no time to recast. Once again, Betty was in the right place at the right time. She even had her own radio show, *The Betty White Show.* It wouldn't last long, but the show's name would be resurrected on TV again . . . and again.

In 1949, Betty was cast as a regular on *Grab Your Phone*, a local weekly Los Angeles TV game show featuring four girls answering phones, or as her father jokingly called it, "Grab Your *What?*" The MC would pose a question, viewers would phone in, and the girls would "grab" the phone. Whoever called with the correct response would win a whopping five dollars! It was not exactly riveting television, but there wasn't a lot else on!

> **Back then, you'd watch anything on that little square box in the corner because it was so novel and new.**

Even if the show wasn't a hit, it caught the attention of disc jockey Al Jarvis, the creator of the *Make Believe Ballroom*, who was in the process of transitioning his hit radio show to television. He couldn't help but notice the charming brunette with the warm demeanor, sweet smile, and quick wit. She'd be perfect for his new show. When Al dialed Betty to offer her the job, she instantly recognized his voice from the radio. Of course, she'd take the job . . . whatever the job was!

She was to be his "girl Friday" on his new daily live television variety show, *Hollywood on Television*, which aired locally on KLAC-TV (now KCOP-TV) in Los Angeles. Even better, he would pay her fifty dollars per week. Back then, television wasn't yet covered by a union, so salaries were set at the discretion—or whim—of the employer. After making ten dollars a week on *Grab Your Phone*, fifty dollars was a fortune. It wasn't so long ago that she had been shelling out money to get experience. Of course, she knew a good opportunity when she saw it and leaped at the chance to join the show—even after she learned it was set to air live six days a week, five hours per day!

Jarvis shared his professional credo with White, and it's one she has followed throughout her career: always consider the audience watching at home. Never talk down to them or over their heads. It is what we love about Betty: that she's smart without being out of touch. She gets it all right without making it look difficult. She's one of us, but she's the best of us.

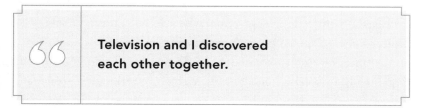

> Television and I discovered each other together.

Fake It 'Til You Make It

The extent of Al's instructions to Betty consisted of: "All you have to do is respond when I talk to you. Just follow where I lead." Nowadays, more preparation is involved in producing a YouTube video. Betty and Al were pretty much winging it, but they had such a natural rapport that the audience didn't seem to notice—or care if things seemed impromptu and a bit slapdash. "When you're on five and a half hours, there's no way to follow a script. We didn't rehearse. I'd slap some makeup on," Betty said of *Hollywood on Television*. Without a script, Betty learned to ad-lib and respond to any situation that might arise, skills that would serve her well for the rest of her career.

Like Betty, Jarvis was a television novice, so they learned the ropes together. Initially, the show stuck close to the radio show format with Betty and Al playing records and bantering between sets. They didn't yet realize that TV isn't just filmed radio! Viewers phoned in and wrote to complain that they wanted to hear what Betty and Al were saying to each other while the records were playing. Message received, loud and clear! One week into the show's run and the pair ditched the records entirely in favor of skits, live performances, and interviews with celebrities.

Through his radio show, Jarvis already had loads of celebrity connections. Before long, any performer who wanted to promote their new project knew to show up at a "special door" at the studio, with Betty and Al interviewing them on air live! Some of the major stars of the day, including songwriters Johnny Mercer and Hoagy Carmichael, singers Sarah Vaughan and Peggy Lee, musician Nat King Cole, and silent film legend Buster Keaton, opened the door . . . and performed on *Hollywood on Television*. And Betty and Al were interviewing them live on television without any advance preparation.

The show was so successful that after three weeks, the station asked them to add another half hour, extending the daily live TV show to a whopping five and a half hours a day! At that point, what difference does another half hour make?! Needless to say, they had no problem filling the time—remember, this was before videotaped commercials, so they had to "perform" live commercials—sometimes as many as fifty-eight a day!

Betty later likened the experience to "television college" and joked that she was Al's "girl Friday . . . as well as Monday through Saturday." Thinking on her feet and filling the air with witty word play for hours a day served to be excellent training for Betty's future career as a game-show contestant and talk-show guest. She was the person you wanted at your party, brightening it up with her effervescent personality and bon mots. Betty always seemed to be having a genuinely good time—and when she was smiling, it was hard not to smile with her.

When Jarvis left the show in 1951 for an opportunity at ABC, a young actor named Eddie Albert temporarily took his place on-air, cohosting with Betty for six months before Hollywood came calling. Albert was offered a plum role in William Wyler's *Roman Holiday* starring Gregory Peck and a pretty young European actress named Audrey Hepburn making her screen debut. Of course, he said yes. The role earned him a Best Supporting Actor Academy Award nomination. He went on to receive another Oscar nomination for Best Supporting Actor for Elaine May's 1972 comedy *The Heartbreak Kid*. He and Betty remained good friends over the years. In 1993, Eddie Albert reunited on-screen with Betty when he played a hotel guest who dates Rose in an episode of *The Golden Girls* spin-off *The Golden Palace*.

With Jarvis and Albert gone, Betty took over as solo host of *Hollywood on Television*, making her (we believe) the first woman to host a TV talk show. Betty had enough energy to fend for herself without a second host. The audience was entranced by her warm and friendly demeanor and her ease in front of the camera. Of course, she was at ease in front of the camera. She'd been performing live on camera for many hours a day many hours a week by then. The camera became her best friend, and everyone watching at home felt that she was their best friend, too. This strong connection with the audience would endure throughout her career.

What Percentage Betty White Are You?

To accurately ascertain what percentage of Betty White you are, answer the below questions honestly, not how you think Betty would answer.

1. In which state do you feel most at home?
   a. New York
   b. Minnesota
   c. Florida
   d. California

2. What's your go-to junk food?
   a. French fries
   b. Red Vines
   c. Hot dogs
   d. All of the above

3. Your secret to life is:
   a. Be nice to people and hope they'll be nice in return.
   b. Get what you can out of people. You've got to look out for #1!
   c. Relax and enjoy yourself. YOLO!
   d. Never stop working!

4. Your idea of fun is:
   a. Playing games with your friends
   b. Going to fancy parties
   c. Going shopping
   d. Watching TV

5. Do you believe in true love?
   a. Absolutely!
   b. True what?
   c. Maybe?
   d. I think so.

6. What's your go-to drink?
   a. Gin and tonic
   b. Margarita
   c. Vodka on the rocks
   d. Rum and Coke

7. Your idea of handsome is:
   a. Paul Newman
   b. Ryan Reynolds
   c. Robert Redford
   d. Denzel Washington

8. You think of yourself as kind of a:
   a. Flirt
   b. Workaholic
   c. Artist
   d. All of the above

9. Your favorite genre of movies is:
   a. Action
   b. Romance
   c. Documentary
   d. Horror

10. Your favorite animal is:
   a. Dogs
   b. Cats
   c. Horses
   d. None

For each question you answered "Betty," you get 10 percent. For every question you answered "Sorta Betty," you get 5 percent. Add up the numbers to figure out what percentage Betty White you are (you can do the math!).

If you got "Betty" on all ten questions, congratulations, **you're 100 percent Betty White!** You're the closest there is to Betty White without actually *being* Betty White. You've certainly got a lot in common with the Golden Girl. You love animals, the Sundance Kid, and romance!

Don't feel too bad if you're not 100 percent Betty White, though. She of all people would want you to be 100 percent yourself.

CHAPTER TWO

BE A PIONEER

IT WAS THE RIGHT TIME AND THE RIGHT place for a multitalented entertainer who was smart enough to say yes to any opportunity—even if it meant learning along the way. That was her specialty—coming through in a clinch and ad-libbing on air, making every flub feel like it had been scripted. While flying solo as host on *Hollywood on Television*, Betty began to develop skits to fill the time.

One regular skit was called "Alvin and Elizabeth," and it featured comic vignettes of a young, married, suburban couple (sort of a precursor to *The Dick Van Dyke Show*, which didn't air for nearly another full decade!), with Betty playing the plucky bride, Elizabeth. These skits made it clear that not only was Betty a talented broadcaster, but she was an actress, a comedian, and an overall entertainer. The skit soon became a fan favorite, and it also attracted the attention of the station manager of KLAC, Don Fedderson, who felt it could be expanded into its own show, a half-hour situation comedy.

"In my wisdom, I said, 'It won't work . . . the jokes won't hold up that long, you can't do a half-hour.' That's how much I knew," said Betty. But she figured it was worth a try. She'd give it a go, along with her *Hollywood on Television* colleagues, writer George Tibbles (who went on to become an Academy Award–nominated composer), and Fedderson (who went on to produce a number of hit shows, including *My Three Sons*). Together, they'd form a production company. They named the new production company Bandy Productions, in honor of Betty's beloved pet Pekingese, Bandit. "We couldn't very well call it Bandit Productions or it would sound like we stole all our material," Betty joked.

For the new series, *Life with Elizabeth*, they cast a young comic actor, Del Moore, as Alvin. He and Betty immediately fell into a comfortable groove. Each episode of the new show was divided into three separate stories, involving the typical comic misunderstandings and foibles in a young married couple's suburban life. You know—guests who refuse to leave a party, salesmen who are too shy to pitch their products, newspapers that land in the front hedge, and bosses who show up for dinner unannounced. Betty's natural ability with physical comedy allowed her to make the most of what was essentially a "housewife" role.

As with *Hollywood on Television*, the new show, which filmed live in front of a studio audience every Saturday night from the Music Hall Theatre in Beverly Hills, relied on White's quick wit and theatrical flair. "You never knew when a camera was gonna break, when a film was gonna break, when you'd have to go out and stand there and talk for five minutes just to fill air time," the show's announcer Jack Narz recalled on PBS's *Betty White: First Lady of Television*. Tibbles would brainstorm story ideas with Betty any chance they got—often during their daily carpools to and from the studio (she was living with her parents!).

Because everything was so hands-on, Betty was able to gain crucial production experience that would serve her well throughout her career. "We didn't hire extra people," she said. "Everybody was doing everything: writing, directing, and producing." Among the show's crew members was a stagehand working his way through film school. His name was Sam Peckinpah, and he went on to become an iconic and iconoclastic director known for incredibly violent, acclaimed films such as *The Wild Bunch* and *Straw Dogs*.

Life with Elizabeth wasn't especially imaginative, as the *New York Times*' Jack Gould noted in his 1954 review. He didn't love the show, but, not surprisingly, he was bowled over by Betty. "What saves the day is Miss White. She has an intuitive feel for farce and delivers her lines, many of them really witty, with an excellent sense of timing. Her style is engagingly offbeat and she imparts to the show an infectious warmth and gay spirit." If NBC was wise, Gould suggested, the Peacock network might even move "the jack-of-all-trades" to prime time. Little did he know that many years later, with *Mama's Family* and *The Golden Girls,* Betty would get more prime-time opportunities on NBC.

> **I had no way of knowing that my lifelong love affair with television had just begun.**

Just like Lucille Ball, whose *I Love Lucy* also stemmed from the "wacky wife" character on a popular radio show (*My Favorite Husband*), Betty was one of the very first women to wield creative power behind the scenes. After airing locally in Los Angeles, the show reached a broader audience in 1953, when it was syndicated nationally. Aside from the fact that it earned White her first of many Emmy Awards (a Regional Los Angeles Emmy in 1952), "Nobody remembers *Life with Elizabeth*. They weren't born when *Life with Elizabeth* was on," Betty joked. Maybe so, but her success with *Life with Elizabeth* was enough to earn her the distinction of honorary mayor of Hollywood in 1955! The future was looking bright.

Betty White's "Firsts"

She was there at the start of TV, and she quickly made a lasting mark. Here are just some of Betty's groundbreaking industry firsts.*

⁎ First woman to produce a national TV show*

⁎ First woman to host a talk show*

⁎ First woman to star in a sitcom*

⁎ First female producer to hire a female director

⁎ First woman to receive an Emmy Award for Outstanding Game Show Host

✳ First (and only) woman to win an Emmy in all of the performing comedy categories: lead, supporting, and guest actress, not to mention game-show host, and a regional Emmy in the '50s for *Life with Elizabeth*.

---

*Or among the very first

I guess I was in television so early that they hadn't discovered that they shouldn't have women in there!

Betty White, Feminist? Sort Of.

Betty came of age before "second-wave" feminism swept the nation's consciousness in the 1960s. Though she never identified as a feminist per se, she never let defined gender roles get in the way of her dreams. As one of the first female TV producers, she was excited to be working with one of the first female TV directors, Betty Turbiville, but she never thought of it as a "feminist" issue. "That was so before the women's movement that I don't think we even thought of it [as a gender issue]," she said. "It was just you did whatever the job was and whatever job you could get." She later joked that though she was "completely in a man's world," she didn't think of it in those terms.

Since it centered around women's friendships and broke down stereotypes about older women, you could say *The Golden Girls'* very existence is a feminist statement. With all of the stories revolving around the women's lives, the program passed the Bechdel Test before the feminist gauge was even created. *Hot in Cleveland*, which also features an ensemble cast of "women of a certain age," also passes the Bechdel Test, and both shows were created by women. "Whether she claims the title or not, Betty White is a feminist role model," according to *Ms.* magazine's Audrey Bilger. "Maybe Betty White doesn't see herself as a feminist, but she plays one on TV."

The Big Time

Pat Weaver, the ad executive who was in charge of NBC, had taken notice of Betty's natural rapport with the audience on *Life with Elizabeth*. "Do you think you can handle doing a half-hour show every day, five days a week?" he asked. Never one to turn down a challenge or an opportunity, Betty responded with an enthusiastic "yes!" That meant she'd be appearing in two nationally broadcast shows, *Life with Elizabeth* and *The Betty White Show*.

She had managed to work five and a half hours a day, six days a week with *Hollywood on Television*, so juggling two half-hour shows was nothing for Betty. In fact, she wondered what she would do with "all the time off!" Even better, she'd be paid a whopping $750 per week for

The Betty White Show. She'd have a bigger production budget, too, with enough money for a five-piece band led by bandleader Frank De Vol, who would go on to become a four-time Academy Award–nominated TV and film composer.

The Betty White Show (the second so far, if you count her earlier radio show) debuted in 1954 with Jack Narz (the future game-show host) introducing the show's sponsors as well as its star. Each episode began with Betty chirping: "It's time to say hello again! And start our show again! And sing a song or two for all of you!" In addition to singing with the orchestra and making chipper chitchat with guests, she'd read viewers' letters, poems, jokes, and stories aloud.

Once again, Betty excelled at thinking on her feet, managing ad-lib commercials, including for diet pills and for a new supplement called Geritol, which promised to boost energy. She told viewers: "To feel stronger fast, I wish you'd give Geritol a try." The vitamin supplement boasted twice the iron in a pound of calf's liver. It also contained about 12 percent alcohol. It was later cited by the Federal Trade Commission for its misleading health claims. But, of course, Betty didn't know that at the time! [The vitamin supplement still exists, but it's entirely different.]

More than half a century after the show ended, on his podcast, Alan Alda asked Betty if she ever drank any Geritol back in the day. She never did. "But maybe I could get rid of the Geritol and just drink the alcohol!" she joked, and they both fell into a warm laughter. Now *that's* the best medicine.

Everything's Coming Up Roses

She's famous for playing one Rose, but Betty has another strong Rose connection. She first covered the Tournament of Roses Parade on New Year's Day in 1955. She happily took on the duty for two decades. She spent every New Year's morning in Pasadena, California, nineteen for NBC and one for CBS, plus six Grand Floral Parades in Portland, Oregon, and ten Macy's Thanksgiving Day Parades in New York. Betty joked, "It got so that if I saw a line of cars waiting for a signal, I had to fight the urge to do a commentary."

LIFE LESSON:

Stand Up for Others

Black tap dancer and singer Arthur Duncan impressed Betty with his talent whenever he performed on *Hollywood on Television*. Once she became a producer of *The Betty White Show*, Betty hired Duncan as a regular to perform a song-and-dance number each episode. But not everyone approved of Duncan's involvement.

As the show expanded nationally, TV stations in the South threatened to pull it from their schedules unless they fired Duncan. "It came as a frightfully ugly surprise, one day, when a few of the stations that carried our show through the South notified us that they would 'with deep regret, find it most difficult to broadcast the program unless Mr. Arthur Duncan was removed from the cast,'" Betty remembered.

"I was shocked, and it goes without saying that Arthur continued to perform on our show as often as possible."

She stood her ground and refused to fire him. "I was livid." She put her foot down and said, "I'm sorry. He stays." Luckily, the network backed up the decision. She got her way. In 1954, that was pretty gutsy. Unfortunately, it didn't solve everything. Initially a ratings success, the show changed time slots and was cancelled before too long. Still, in addition to earning Betty her first Emmy, it helped launch Duncan's career. And she never made a big deal about what she had done.

In fact, Duncan was unaware of the controversy surrounding his appearance and Betty's efforts to stand up for him until many years later. Duncan credited Betty with giving him his start in show business. His experience working on *The Betty White Show* led to a regular gig on *The Lawrence Welk Show* for almost twenty years, making him the first African American regular on a variety show. In 2017, Duncan and White reunited on the series premiere of the Steve Harvey reality talent series *Little Big Shots: Forever Young*, in which they performed a dance together for the first time in more than fifty years.

BETTY WHITE TRIVIA: Betty was not only there for the beginning of TV but also for the introduction of color TV. She remembers the day in 1954 when she first saw a color TV image. NBC invited her to a private demonstration of color television on their lot in Burbank. "It was mind-boggling," Betty said. The crowd watched as the black-and-white image of bacon and eggs sizzled in the pan. "Suddenly, it switched to color before our eyes, and the gasp that went up could be heard all over Burbank."

A Date with the Angels

Along with *Life with Elizabeth* and *I Love Lucy*, *A Date with the Angels*, which aired on ABC in 1957, was one of the first network attempts of a "domestic" situation comedy. Betty starred as daydreaming new bride Vickie Angel whose dream sequences were incorporated into the story line. Her insurance salesman husband, Gus Angel, was played by veteran actor Bill Williams, who Betty knew from radio and local TV.

When the show's sponsor, Plymouth, objected to the female-oriented "dream" component, the network had them cut. But without the fantasy element, the show lacked spark or originality. Betty later said it was the only time she had ever wanted to get out of a contract. ABC agreed the show wasn't working, but Betty still had thirteen weeks remaining on her contract, and they wouldn't let her out early. So ABC nixed Williams and renamed the show *The Betty White Show*, which was basically a reboot of her previous live daytime talk/variety show by the same name (don't worry, it's hard to keep track!). Even though the new incarnation of *The Betty White Show* disappointed in the ratings, Betty once again proved her versatility. A scripted filmed sitcom not clicking with the audience? No worries. I'll just invite some of my celebrity friends on to entertain and have a good time until my contract runs out. Leave it to Betty to turn a disappointment into an opportunity, something she'd do again and again throughout her career.

Everyone Loves Betty White

Everyone's wild about Betty, not just you and me, but also other celebrities who are vocal in their admiration for America's first lady of television.

Here are some of the things they've said about the incomparable Ms. White:

"No matter what character she plays, Betty White is always funny, always smart, and always at least a little sexy . . . If you happen to run into Betty White, tell her thank you. I'd like to be like her one day."

—Lauren Graham

"Betty White has shown audiences she isn't just sweet, she's sassy."

—Katie Couric

"She has become an American institution. I have to bend my knee every time I run into her, and I'm getting tired of it!"

—Ed Asner

"If you pass 70, just look to Betty and that's the way to do it!"

—Valerie Harper

"She can be both tender and sweet, and empathetic to people who are going through times that are tough. She can be just outrageously funny and get you out of a blue mood. She's a very special woman."

—Mary Tyler Moore

"She's funny and she's bawdy. She sings and she's a great actress and a good friend."

—Carol Burnett

"She's one of the smartest, funniest, kindest, most generous women … in a business that doesn't normally have that kind of people."

—Valerie Bertinelli

"When I think of Betty White, who she really is, is that big open smile."

—Rue McClanahan

"Betty White is one of the few people who walks into the room and you know her. You've known her all your life. For some reason, she's one of those people who's always welcome."

—Carl Reiner

"You kinda get the sense from Betty that she is extremely, wickedly sexy, but at the same time, she knows how to navigate a church social. That's unusual, and why comics and actors and directors love her so much. It has an air of naughtiness that I think people find irresistible."

—Craig Ferguson

"Jay-Z was excited about the idea of working with Betty White— further proof that her influence is pervasive and enormous."

—Lorne Michaels

"I just want to have fun like Betty White."

—Queen Latifah

"She's captured our hearts while she tickled our funny bones for decades."

—Alan Alda

"She's this incredibly authentic, charming, talented, funny woman. You can put somebody who's as multifaceted as Betty in any situation. Because of that, she's always going to be relevant. She's always going to be of the moment. That's what makes her really special. She is this lovable character with an edge."

—Ryan Reynolds

CHAPTER THREE

LUCK AND LOVE

SHE'S BEEN CALLED "THE FIRST LADY OF game shows," a "game-show goddess," and "the most prolific game-show panelist in TV history." With good reason. Betty was a game-show pioneer. Beginning with *Grab Your Phone* in 1949, she appeared on more than fifty game shows throughout the years as both a game player and an expert panelist. Her quick retorts, warm smile, and bawdy humor helped make Betty a fan favorite (as well as a game-show producer's go-to choice). Fiercely competitive, she played to win. And to show audiences a good time, of course.

"Betty was very good, almost always had the right answers," said Mark Goodson, half of the mega-successful game-show partnership

Goodson-Todman Productions (the force behind *The Price Is Right*, *Family Feud*, *The Match Game*, *Password*, and many more shows). She was such a natural, Goodson-Todman hired Betty as a guest on most of their shows for more than four decades. Betty "was never at a loss for words, and in our business, words are worth a lot," said Goodson.

> 66 **Where else can you spend a couple of hours playing games with nice people and get paid for it?**

BETTY WHITE TRIVIA: Betty is not only the reigning Game-Show Queen, but she's also legendary as a talk-show host and guest. She served as the go-to talk-show guest and replacement host for decades. She was a recurring regular with more than seventy appearances on *Tonight Starring Jack Paar* (later called *The Jack Paar Tonight Show*) and appeared on *The Merv Griffin Show* and *The Tonight Show Starring Johnny Carson*. She was good friends with all three hosts and filled in for them occasionally. They knew the audience was in good hands with Betty. She'd be sure to keep the fun going.

In one famous skit on *The Tonight Show Starring Johnny Carson* in 1979, the talk-show host plays Adam to White's Eve "twenty years later" and in the middle of marital troubles. Wearing skin-colored garments made to appear semi-naked, the pair had green leaves to hide their "private areas." Or as Betty put it, the costumes consisted of "a few strategically placed" fig leaves and a long, blonde wig. Another episode had the pair dressed in skimpy leopard costumes as Tarzan and Jane "twenty years later," with Jane asking for a divorce.

Since most game shows filmed in New York back then, Betty would often time her appearances to coincide with a visit to *The Jack Paar Tonight Show*.

Betty called game shows "the best training in the world" because you have to think quickly on your feet—something she already excelled at. She radiates a special blend of intelligence and joy that audiences love. As a result, anytime she had a lull in her career over the years, she could rely on game shows to keep her working. "Game shows became a mainstay for me, not only because I could use the work and the exposure but because they were just plain fun to do and kept me in touch with so many friends," Betty said.

Though she, no doubt, realized that some classically trained actors viewed game-show appearances as a step down from serious roles, Betty didn't care about the stigma. Well, maybe she cared a little bit because she penned an essay, "Game Shows Are a Refreshing Change of Pace," which was syndicated in newspapers in 1964. "It is a delight to make one's living playing games like *To Tell the Truth*, *The Match Game*, *Password*, and *Get the Message*, but I always bristle a little when people get that supercilious tone when they mention 'game shows,'" she wrote. Go, Betty! I love that she's not afraid to embrace "low brow" culture.

On NPR, Linda Holmes called Betty "probably the best game-show guest celebrity who ever lived." We agree, Ms. Holmes! Below, we run through some of the most memorable shows—and especially, winning moments:

Make the Connection

After *Grab Your Phone*, Betty's next game-show appearance was on Goodson-Todman's *Make the Connection*, hosted by Gene Rayburn (who replaced Jim McKay, who went on to be an ABC Sports host). *Make the Connection* was short-lived (only thirteen episodes), but it's noteworthy because Rayburn went on to host the popular game show *The Match Game* in its various incarnations for more than two decades. Not surprisingly, Betty was frequently a guest!

What's My Line?

What's My Line?, which premiered in 1950, was one of the earliest game shows on TV. The panel show presented contestants with unusual occupations, and then celebrity panelists would ask a series of "yes" or "no" questions in order to determine the contestant's profession. Every episode featured a celebrity "mystery guest," and over the years, Sean Connery, Julie Andrews, Lauren Bacall, B.B. King, Groucho Marx, Salvador Dalí, Walt Disney, Clint Eastwood, Duke Ellington, Jane Fonda, Gene Hackman, Barbra Streisand, and so many more stars played that role. White's first appearance on the show in 1955 showcased her natural charm and quick wit. Even though she never won, she was invited back several times over the years, including several times with her husband, Allen Ludden.

To Tell the Truth

Betty appeared as a panelist on most of the incarnations of *To Tell the Truth* beginning in 1961 and up until 2016, when the classic game show was revived by Anthony Anderson (*black-ish*). The basic premise is that one of the three contestants is "real" while the others are imposters. Celebrity guests, such as Betty White, had to ask questions to determine who the "real" person was. In 1963, Betty appeared on the show with her new husband, Allen Ludden. When the host asked how long the couple had been married, Betty responded immediately: "Three weeks, three days, four hours, and twenty minutes." "You mean forty minutes," Allen teased. But who's counting?

When Anderson decided to bring the show back, he knew there was one person he had to have on: "the lovely and talented Miss Betty White." Anderson noted that Betty had appeared on *To Tell the Truth* more than fifty times over fifty years. "No one has played this game better," said Anderson. So true!

BETTY WHITE TRIVIA: After appearing on the original *Password,* which was hosted by her husband, Allen Ludden, White went on to appear on all three updated versions of the game show over the years: *Password Plus*, *Super Password*, and *Million Dollar Password*, which means she appeared with all five hosts of the series—Ludden, Bill Cullen, Tom Kennedy, Bert Convy, and Regis Philbin.

The Match Game

Thanks to its rotating celebrity panel of gabbers, *The Match Game* felt more like a talk show than a game show. Among the regulars were snarky wits including Charles Nelson Reilly, Brett Somers, and, of course, Betty White. Over the years, Betty appeared on the show hundreds of times, occasionally with Allen.

"A word would come up and the contestant would have to match that word," Betty remembered. In one episode, the word requiring a "match" was "weeping." "There was weeping willow, pussy willow and tit willow, and well, we came up with 'weeping,' 'pussy,' and 'tit.' It was a showstopper, but it worked!" Leave it to Betty to push the envelope . . . on a game show!

Jeopardy!

Believe it or not, Betty has never appeared on the iconic game show, but she is a self-professed *Jeopardy!* fan, telling the *New York Post* in 2018 that she loves the game and also has "a huge crush on the host, Alex Trebek." The feeling was clearly mutual. It wasn't a coincidence that Trebek made guest appearances as himself on two of White's shows: *Golden Girls* and years later on *Hot in Cleveland*. Before he died in 2020, Trebek half-jokingly suggested that his old friend Betty White would make for the ideal host to replace him on *Jeopardy!* He told *Good Morning America*, "They want somebody younger, somebody funnier, she checks all those boxes."

Hollywood Squares

As with *The Match Game*, *Password*, and *To Tell the Truth*, this popular show (which initially premiered in 1966) was revived in various incarnations over the years—and Betty was usually involved. The game show featured two contestants competing in a game of Tic-Tac-Toe, with celebrities seated at desks in open-faced cubes arranged like a Tic-Tac-Toe board. Betty was among the regular "squares," and when the show relaunched as *The New Hollywood Squares* in 1986, Betty once again had a square to call her own.

Liar's Club

When this game show first launched in 1969, Rod Serling (of *The Twilight Zone* fame) was the host, which was enough to pique Betty's interest. The show featured a panel of celebrity guests who provided unusual "facts" about various objects, and contestants had to determine who was telling the truth. Serling only lasted as host for a year before being replaced by Bill Armstrong. In 1974, Betty was invited to be a regular panel member of the show, which was being produced at KTTV, a local television station where, conveniently, Allen taped his syndicated talk/variety show called *Ludden Unlimited*. Before long, Bill Armstrong was soon replaced by none other than . . . Allen Ludden! Got that straight?

Just Men!

For decades, Betty's agents tried to pitch her as a game-show host without success. The TV networks (there were only three back then!) insisted that female viewers wanted to see male hosts and that they preferred "authoritative male sounds!" By 1983, times had changed— sort of—and NBC offered Betty the job of host on a new TV show *Just Men!*

Featuring an all-male slate of "celebrity panelists" (including '70s TV stars such as Mr. T, John Ritter, and David Hasselhoff), it was

Betty's first and only time hosting a game show. Two female contestants tried to compete to see who could better predict the men's answers to a variety of questions. It was a novel idea—but not necessarily a good one!

The *Washington Post*'s Tom Shales lamented that White, a generally terrific comedian, "is terribly demeaned by this role, which has her hobbling about from man to man as they utter answers or remarks that are supposedly uproarious." He went so far as to call *Just Men!* "the litmus test for people who think the TV show that can make them physically ill hasn't been invented." White was much more diplomatic when she said, "*Just Men!* was a short but interesting little adventure." Way to look on the bright side, as usual, Betty!

Actually, there was a bright side to *Just Men!*: though it only aired for thirteen weeks, the show earned Betty an Emmy Award, making her the first female to win the Emmy for Outstanding Game Show Host (it would be more than two decades for another woman to win that award, when Meredith Vieira won for hosting the syndicated version of *Who Wants to Be a Millionaire* in 2005). Once again, somehow Betty turned a disappointment into a success!

LIFE LESSON:

Hold Out for True Love— On Your Own Terms

Betty took a chance on love twice with two brief "practice marriages" before finding the real thing. She knew enough not to settle in a relationship that wasn't working for her. That's a big deal, considering back then divorce was considered scandalous—and she was, after all, considered America's Sweetheart for a time. Leave it to Betty not to worry about any backlash and to follow her heart without hurting her career. Lucky for her that smartphones and social media were still many years off!

She met her first husband, chicken farmer Dick Barker, during World War II at one of the dances she attended as a volunteer with the American Women's Voluntary Services (AWVS) in Los Angeles. He proposed to her before heading overseas, and they exchanged love letters throughout the war. After the war ended and he returned home and ... how could Betty refuse him? They married, but after four months on Barker's rural Ohio chicken farm, Betty knew she had made a mistake. She later said they married because they wanted to sleep together. "It lasted six months, and we were in bed for six months!" She returned to Los Angeles and her career. (Luckily, her folks were always super-supportive and were more than happy to welcome her and her dog, Bandy, to live with them in their Brentwood home.)

She met her second husband, agent Lane Allen, when he showed up to scout new talent at the Bliss-Hayden when Betty was starring in their latest production. He was so impressed by her talent—and her beauty—that he came backstage after the show to introduce himself. She was instantly smitten. He asked her out, and they soon became a regular item, culminating in marriage in 1947. She was "deeply in love," but when he pressured her to give up her career two years after they married (presumably to pop out some kids), it was a deal-breaker. "When you have a calling, you have to follow it, so I made the choice, blew the marriage, and I've never regretted it," she said about her second marriage.

Marriage was never the goal for her. She was looking for love— and someone who would be supportive rather than competitive of her career. Clearly, her first two husbands weren't able to fulfill those needs. Rather than stick around out of a sense of duty, she knew it was better to be alone than to stay with the wrong person. And she certainly wasn't going to give up her big Hollywood dreams to fulfill some man's fantasy of a wife. "Both marriages helped me to appreciate the real thing when it came along," she said.

In the 2018 PBS special, *Betty White: First Lady of Television*, the actress recalled falling in love with silver-haired, bespectacled Allen Ludden when she appeared as a guest on his game show, *Password*, in 1961, just three weeks after it first went on the air. "The host was very nice and very attractive, and I thought, 'Ooh!'" She even flirted on-air. When Ludden asked: "What are your plans for the summer, Betty?" she suggestively asked: "What did you have in mind, Allen?"

Sparks didn't fly between them until 1962, when they did summer stock theater together in Cape Cod, playing a married couple in the romantic comedy *Critic's Choice*. At the end of the third act of the play, loose ends are tied up and the couple share a final kiss before the curtain drops. One night, Allen held the kiss longer than usual—and Betty's boyfriend at the time noticed the chemistry between them. Betty soon realized she had developed feelings for the widower, who had lost his wife, Margaret, to cancer the prior year. She broke up with the poor, perceptive guy she had been dating at the time and dove full force into her transcontinental love affair with Allen.

They were well matched in temperament, intelligence, and wit, and Allen proposed marriage, but after two divorces, Betty was reluctant to jump into a third marriage. Besides, the lifelong California girl was hesitant to move to New York, where Ludden taped *Password* and lived with his children. Allen wasn't giving up so easily. He wore the engagement ring he had used to propose on a gold chain around his neck, saying he'd keep it on until she agreed to marry. On Easter, Allen sent Betty a stuffed white bunny wearing gold earrings adorned with tiny diamonds, rubies, and sapphires, along with a note that read: "Please say YES." Betty called right away and said YES. "It wasn't the earrings that did it," Betty said later. "It was the goddamned bunny. I still have it." It's a sweet story, but the truth is even sweeter: Even before the bunny arrived, Betty had come to the conclusion that she was head over heels in love with Allen and didn't want to spend another day apart.

Because Allen couldn't get extra vacation time off *Password*—and because he didn't want to let another moment pass before marrying Betty and California had a three-day waiting period, the couple eloped. They had a civil ceremony at the Sands Hotel in Las Vegas on June 14, 1963, with only Allen's children and Betty's parents in attendance. They returned to New York from their wedding-honeymoon trip and immediately went directly from the airport to the CBS studio to tape *Password*. "Playing it a little close, wouldn't you say?"

A lifelong Californian, Betty agreed to move with Allen and his children to a house in suburban Westchester County outside of New York City. He had to be in commuting distance of the studio, and they didn't want to uproot the kids. Betty continued to appear on *Password* after they were married. Audiences liked to feel as though they were eavesdropping on the couple's romantic banter. Betty was such a pro that nobody would dare suggest she relied on nepotism to get work. "She was already the best player we had. Betty was just a rock on our show, and every viewer knew it," said Mike Gargiulo, who directed the 1963 episode where Betty appeared on the show as a newlywed.

During one episode of *Password*, Ludden asks his wife if she has a philosophy when it comes to games. Her response is classic Betty: "I love games, and I love game shows. I think it is a good mental exercise and keeps everyone alert and on their toes," she said, adding sheepishly: "And you meet a lot of husbands that way!"

Five years later, with the kids out of the house, the couple moved to California, where *Password* had been relocated. Betty would forever remain a California girl, and Allen was quick to adapt to the relaxed California lifestyle. They enjoyed many happy years there together, hosting game night with friends. Sounds dull, unless your friends include Burt Reynolds, Rock Hudson, Fred Astaire, Mel Brooks and Anne Bancroft, Carl Reiner, and Clint Eastwood! Betty said they "played for blood" with "girls against boys." Some nights, they'd play "murder" at Carol Burnett's house, where one member of the group is the designated "killer" and the rest of the guests have to find out who it is—before they're "killed." Imagine playing "Murder" with the cast of *The Carol Burnett Show*!

Just as they were planning to build their dream vacation home in Carmel, California, Allen was diagnosed with terminal stomach cancer. "We decided to move on and make the most of every day for whatever time we had together," Betty said. Allen lived long enough to see the house finished, but got the chance to sleep there for only two nights before his death on June 9, 1981, just a few days before the couple's eighteenth wedding anniversary. White has often repeated that her only regret in life was that she didn't accept Ludden's proposal sooner. "I spent a whole year, wasted a whole year, that Allen and I could have had together," she told Oprah in 2015.

Betty kept Allen's memory close throughout the years. "Sure, you miss the love of your life," she said. "The person isn't around anymore. But with a good attitude, you can keep them a lot closer than you would if you just let it all go and turned into grief," she said. Anytime she played a widow on-screen, she'd always conjure up memories of

Allen. When Rose Nylund talked about missing her beloved late husband, Charlie, on *The Golden Girls*, you could see Betty turning wistful thinking of Allen. Off-screen, Betty said that every once in a while she'd find herself saying "good morning" to Allen's picture.

Betty has dated sporadically over the years, but, as she told Anderson Cooper in 2011, she has never felt any desire to walk down the aisle again. "I had the love of my life," she said. Besides, she's always preferred older men. "Unfortunately, today I don't think there is anyone older than I am!"

If you've had the best, who needs the rest?

Betty's Rules for a Happy Relationship:

✳ **Be true equals.** Betty said that Allen was more than a husband and a friend. They supported each other's professional endeavors. They were a team, always looking out for each other.

✳ **Be flexible.** Betty hadn't planned on getting married a third time, and she wasn't counting on being a stepmother or moving to New York. But she knew that true love doesn't strike often, and when it does, you sometimes have to move Heaven and Earth—or at least temporarily move to New York City.

* **Be honest, but gentle.** Allen would give honest, supportive feedback, and Betty tried to do the same in return. Betty felt honesty was crucial, but that doesn't mean you've got to be blunt in your delivery. "Being frank is fine, but not to the point of brutality," Betty said.

* **Don't let the little things get to you.** Everyone has annoying habits and makes occasional mistakes. Overlook those little annoyances and be like Betty. Emphasize the positive. Easier said than done, we know. Try a simple tip Betty has shared: If you're tempted to say something you may later regret, leave the room and take a deep breath.

LIFE LESSON:

Sometimes "No" Is the Right Answer

Betty always jumped at a chance to test out her chops at something new, but she also knew when to say no. She knew it wasn't a good opportunity if it wasn't the right fit. In the early 1970s, Betty's agent got a call from NBC. They were looking for a "new girl" on *Today*, and they wanted the girl with the golden smile for the job. By any measure, it would be a plum gig (high visibility, good pay), but she knew it would be an exhausting endeavor—especially since the morning show was based in New York and she was a dedicated California girl.

NBC sweetened the deal and made it hard for her to turn down— even offering to put her up in her own suite at the swanky St. Regis

Hotel in Manhattan and fly her home to California every weekend, if she wanted. Even someone with her amazing energy level knew that the cross-country commute would be too much. She considered NBC's generous offer, but in her gut she knew she wouldn't be happy spending so much time in the air.

"The final answer was no. It's not easy to see a grown agent cry," she said later. "Poor NBC was stuck with a gal named Barbara Walters, and they somehow managed to muddle through!"

Though her agent at the time thought she was nuts, Betty never had any regrets about turning down the gig. For Betty, "the life you live is always more important than the job you do. And place has always been terribly important to me," she said in an interview with the Television Academy.

One of the many things we love about Betty is that she makes life choices that work for her and lives life without regrets (see below).

LIFE LESSON:

Choose Your Own Path

When Betty was coming of age, there was very little discussion of "choosing motherhood." It was assumed that all girls wanted to get married and have children—and then stay home to be a housewife. But Betty knew early on that she wanted to pursue a career in show business—and she didn't want anything to get in the way of that. Barbara Walters once asked her if she had ever wanted a child, and Betty said plainly that she had never seriously considered it. For someone of her generation to even think such a thing—let alone say it aloud on TV—was intrepid.

"I know there are many career girls today who would disagree, but I'm not a big believer in being able to do both. I think somebody takes the short end of the stick," Betty said. As an overachiever and a self-proclaimed workaholic, "I didn't think I could do justice to both career and motherhood." But she acknowledged, "It's such an individual choice. And I'm a stepmother. I have the best stepchildren in the world."

When she and Allen first married, she was suddenly the step-mother of three, David, Martha, and Sarah. "We got along great. So great, they called me 'Dragon Lady,' lovingly. Even after all these years, we love each other dearly, and I am most proud of the children this career girl inherited!"

Now that "child-free" is actually a term—and a movement—Betty is considered to be the unofficial patron saint. In 2019, she was featured in *Glamour* magazine alongside other Hollywood stars who opted to forgo motherhood, including Oprah Winfrey, Jennifer Aniston, and Ellen DeGeneres. The article noted that "America's grandma isn't actually a grandma, in case you didn't know."

> I love children. The only problem with children is they grow up to be people, and I just like animals better than people. It's that simple.

BETTY WHITE TRIVIA: Betty White and Allen Ludden were such a well-known celebrity couple at the time that they played themselves in an episode of *The Odd Couple* in 1972. In the episode, Felix Unger (Tony Randall) and Oscar Madison (Jack Klugman) appear on an episode of *Password*, hosted by Ludden, with White as their competitor. Things don't go well when Felix has a panic attack and refuses to accept he lost. In real life, actors Tony Randall and Jack Klugman, good friends of Betty and Allen's, regularly appeared on *Password*.

CHAPTER FOUR

DO WHAT YOU LOVE
(AND LOVE A LOT!)

SHE'S GONE SO FAR AS TO SAY SHE PREFERS
the company of animals to the company of most people, and who can
blame her? "Animals don't lie. Animals don't criticize," wrote White in
her 2011 memoir, *If You Ask Me (And of Course You Won't)*. "If animals have
moody days, they handle them better than humans do." So true!

Throughout her life, she's devoted many thousands of hours and
dollars to supporting animal causes. "I stay in show business to pay for
my animal business. It's that simple," Betty told Katie Couric in 2017.
She was only half-joking. She explained: "They just fascinate me, and I
adore them. I love to touch them. I love to hold them. I love to see them.
They just comfort me." We get it, Betty!

Maybe because she's so comfortable around them, Betty has always enjoyed a special connection with animals. "They love you so much, and they communicate with you so much, you've got to keep reading them because they read you like a book," she said. She confessed that she's always talked to her pets as if they were human. "I couldn't care less if I am considered weird by the uninitiated; it works. If animals are simply dealt into the conversation instead of talked down to, they may not understand the exact words, but they soon learn to pick up on some pretty subtle meanings. Their radar systems are far superior to our own," she said.

In 2012, CNN's Piers Morgan asked Betty White what the greatest moment of her life was, aside from her marriage to Allen. Her answer? "The hour and a half I spent in the cage with Koko, the signing gorilla," she said. White met the famous gorilla in 2004, and the two became fast friends, connecting a number of times over the years. Of their first visit, White told Morgan: "I sat down opposite her. I had my hands on her fat tummy. I was in there for about an hour and a half. It was maybe one of the most magical moments of my entire life," Betty recalled. By the time she visited again, Koko had even made up a special nickname for Betty: "Lipstick."

When Koko died in 2018, Betty mourned her animal friend on Twitter, writing, "I treasure every minute we spent together."

LIFE LESSON:
Combine Your Passions

Rather than keep her love of animals and her love of performing separate, Betty managed to combine her two passions and incorporate animals into her showbiz career. She added critters to whatever show she was on, starting with a section devoted to puppies on *Hollywood on Television*. One day, the show's producer sent a Saint Bernard puppy on to the set as a surprise gift for Betty. "Of course, the show went to hell in a handbasket," Betty remembered. But, in a good way! Betty happily adopted the dog, which she named Stormy, and her costar Del Moore adopted Stormy's brother, which Del named Wellington. The new pets were worked into the story line on *Life with Elizabeth*, with Alvin and Elizabeth surprising each other with Saint Bernard puppies!

After falling in love with a baby elephant who appeared in a dream sequence on *Life with Elizabeth*, Betty decided to bring the baby elephant onto *Hollywood on Television*. She was so crazy about the elephant that she tried to convince NBC to buy the animal! Her pitch? "It would also be a comfortable, safe home for the little/big girl and sensational publicity for NBC—forget the peacock!" Alas, NBC passed on the idea, and the executive she pitched let Betty down easy. Though he said that he, too, loved elephants, "purchasing one didn't quite fit into the network's game plan, somehow," Betty recalled.

Perhaps she's so smitten with animals because Betty is half-animal, herself:

> **It is an absolute fact that I should not be allowed out without a keeper of my own.**

Among her many writings are several essays and books on the topic of animals, including *Betty White's Pet-Love: How Pets Take Care of Us* (1983), about the bond between humans and their companion animals; *Betty & Friends: My Life at the Zoo* (2011), a scrapbook of her favorite zoo animals, including Gita the elephant and Bruno the orangutan, along with photographs and colorful anecdotes; and *The Leading Lady: Dinah's Story* (1991), which she cowrote with her friend, writer and actor Tom Sullivan. *The Leading Lady* describes how Dinah, a guide dog, gave Sullivan, blind since birth, his first taste of independence and how White took Dinah in when she "retired" from doing her job.

Starting early on in her career with *Hollywood on Television* and *Life with Elizabeth*, Betty always tried to involve pets in whatever show she was doing. Here are some of her most memorable shows involving animals:

The Pet Set

The series nearest and dearest to Betty's heart is one of her shortest-lived and perhaps the least remembered: *The Pet Set*, a weekly syndicated show featuring celebrities and their pets. Executive produced by her beloved husband, Allen Ludden, who also served as announcer, the syndicated series hit the air in 1971 and was picked up by 110 cities around the country.

Her guests included some of the biggest showbiz stars of the day: James Brolin, James Stewart, Doris Day, Burt Reynolds, Shirley Jones, Vincent Price, Della Reese, Michael Landon, Barbara Eden, Lorne Greene, Mary Tyler Moore, and many more. These were big names back in the day! And they weren't even promoting a new movie or TV show, which is generally the case nowadays with A-listers appearing on a talk show. They just came on the show because Betty invited them. And they got to bring their pet! And it sounded like fun!

Though *The Pet Set* focused primarily on household pets such as dogs and cats, all varieties of wild animals appeared on the show, including lions, elephants, wolves, bears, water buffalos, cheetahs, penguins, seals, eagles, and more. Amazingly, with all of those wild animals and household pets wandering around the set, there were never any accidents! Unfortunately, the show didn't catch on and was cancelled due to low ratings before long. Even though it wasn't a hit, it was perhaps Betty's all-time favorite TV experience. "It was the happiest I've ever been on television," she said. "I felt like a kid in a candy store."

In 2021, to commemorate the fiftieth anniversary of *The Pet Set* (and Betty's ninety-ninth birthday!), the long unseen series, now rebranded *Betty White's Pet Set*, became available on digital platforms and DVD. "If I haven't told you already, I will now. *The Pet Set* is one of my favorite shows. I'm thrilled it's going to be seen again after all these years," Betty said in a press release.

The Golden Girls

Like Betty, Rose, *The Golden Girls* character she played, was a fierce animal lover—and she, too, believed she had a special connection with them. Rose's St. Olaf stories always seemed to involve a farm animal or two. Remember all the times she reminisced about taking care of Larry, her one-eyed pig?! Some of the most memorable episodes of *The Golden Girls* involve animals, and the actress's love for animals is apparent in every scene she shares with her furry friends.

In fact, were it not for a little gray kitty, Rose may never have met her housemates. In a flashback, we learn that after Blanche's husband died, she posted an ad looking for housemates on the bulletin board at the local grocery store (pre-Craigslist and Facebook!). Rose was looking for a new place to live because her landlord kicked her out because of her cat, Mr. Peepers. At first, Blanche dismisses Rose as just a flaky "cat person"—and who could blame her? Rose is clutching Mr. Peepers as she boasts about being a "wild woman" because she eats raw cookie dough, but her kindness and generosity (she gives the cat to a little boy) wins Blanche over. Blanche asks Rose to move in with her, and the rest is history!

In season one, when Dorothy is about to call the exterminator on a "rat" she finds in the kitchen, Rose urges her to reconsider. "I can communicate with animals," she boasts to Dorothy. "He's just a little field mouse who's lost his way. He'll listen to me. Mice always have." But when he doesn't listen to Rose, she tells Dorothy, "This mouse is an odd duck." Later in the episode, when Dorothy tries talking to the mouse herself, it seems to work. Rose cautions her that communicating with animals is "a powerful gift" and urges her to "use it wisely." Again, that's Betty talking!

In the series' final season, as a birthday gift, Rose's friends get her a dog named Jake. She brings Jake on her candy striper rounds at the hospital where she volunteers. An elderly couple immediately connects with Jake. By the end of the episode, the wife has passed away and the husband is grieving the loss. Just as she did with the kitten in season one, Betty gives away her beloved pet to try to comfort someone else in need. Once again, through Rose, Betty White is sharing her passion for animals and her compassion for people.

The Golden Palace

White used her role on *The Golden Girls* spin-off *The Golden Palace* to champion an organization that rescues retired greyhounds. The episode, "A New Leash on Life," has Blanche dating a greyhound breeder, who is staying at the Golden Hotel. But when Rose learns what will happen to a particular greyhound if it doesn't win the next race, she's heartbroken. When the greyhound loses the race and is going to be put to sleep, Rose announces that she will make sure it finds a home. The episode was intended as a way to educate the audiences—and boy did it.

The National Greyhound Adoption program had only recently been founded, and they were pleasantly surprised to learn—after the fact—that they would be mentioned on the hit program. The program's website reads:

> "Betty White's character stepped up and said, something to the effect of, 'I'm sending this greyhound to the National Greyhound Adoption Program where it will be safe.' You could have knocked us over with a feather! We had no idea we would be mentioned in the episode!"

The following January at the North American Veterinary Conference, the nonprofit presented White with a framed print with an engraved plate commemorating the event and honoring her. Way to make a difference with your work!

Hot in Cleveland

While no animals actually appear in "Two Girls and a Rhino," the season three episode gives Betty White's Elka an opportunity to talk about her love of animals and the importance of zoos and animal preservation. When Victoria (Wendie Malick) does a TV segment about the endangered black rhinos who refuse to mate at the Cleveland Zoo, the zookeeper discovers that the mixture of Elka's and Joy's (Jane Leeves) pheromones serves as an aphrodisiac!

Like Betty, the prickly Elka seems to like animals more than people. While Joy panics when she learns she'll have to stay at the zoo for three days so the rhinos can mate, Elka is thrilled to be sleeping on a cot in the zoo with the animals. Elka is so at home at the zoo, she communicates with the animals, chirping back to the birds as if they could understand her. Joy is skeptical: "I know you consider yourself some Dr. Dolittle, but you can't possibly expect them to respond." And right then, as if on cue, crows reply to Elka's caw.

"What is it with you and animals?" Joy finally asks.

"They were here first. We hunt them for sport. We destroy their natural habitat," Elka explains. When Joy points out that animals seem to love Elka, she responds: "They don't love me. They just love, and that love is the purest, most joyous thing in the world." That sounds like Betty talking!

In honor of Betty's love of animals, the crew of *Hot in Cleveland* adopted a baby orangutan at the Los Angeles Zoo in her name. Fittingly, they named her Elka.

Support Causes Close to Your Heart

There are so many nonprofit organizations devoted to animal welfare and other worthy causes. Here are just a few of the many organizations Betty has supported throughout the years:

BRAVEHEARTS:

This Illinois-based therapeutic riding program serves both children and adults. It's also the largest horse program in the United States for military families. Betty spoke about how the medical community has come to acknowledge the benefits of therapeutic riding programs. "Doctors write prescriptions for patients that they think the best thing in the world that would help them more than any medication is to get a pet," she said.

www.braveheartsriding.org

GUIDE DOGS FOR THE BLIND:

Betty sponsored a guide dog every Christmas, and she did a public service announcement (PSA) about the nonprofit organization Guide Dogs for the Blind. In the PSA, which aired nationally, she's cuddling Rhett, "a puppy with a very special job, being a guide dog for someone who is blind." Betty knew a lot about guide dogs through her friend and cowriter Tom Sullivan, who was blind from birth and used guide dogs (including Dinah) for support.

www.guidedogs.com

MORRIS ANIMAL FOUNDATION:

The Denver-based nonprofit organization, which funds veterinary research, has been one of Betty's favorite causes for more than fifty years! On behalf of her work as a longtime trustee, the organization established the Betty White Wildlife Rapid Response Fund, which helps fund research on wildlife health needs in times of crisis, such as environmental disasters. "Everyone knows how much I love dogs and cats, but wildlife species have a special place in my heart, too," said White.

In 2011, White, then eighty-eight, hammed it up, posing with oiled-up shirtless male beefcakes for a Betty White "pinup" calendar dedicated to raising money (and awareness) for the Morris Animal Foundation. The things you have to do for a good cause! But Betty, as always, was more than willing to make the "sacrifice."

www.morrisanimalfoundation.org

THE LOS ANGELES ZOO:

Whenever Betty traveled to a different city to shoot a movie, she'd try to visit the local zoo and see her animal friends. What better way to feel at home in a city than by surrounding herself with her beloved animals? While filming in New Mexico, she swung by the Albuquerque Zoo. If she was shooting in Atlanta, she'd be sure to visit both Zoo Atlanta and the Georgia Aquarium. "No matter where it may be, I will never come away from a zoo visit without having seen something or learned something to remember," she wrote in *Betty & Friends: My Life at the Zoo.*

She's been a member of the board of directors at the Los Angeles Zoo since 1974 and has donated many thousands of dollars—and time—to the organization. In 2010, White took ABC News' *Nightline* on a personal tour of what she called her "second home," the Los Angeles Zoo. "I've been around so long, they can't get rid of me," she joked about the zoo, where she has volunteered for four decades as a trustee, fund-raiser, and all-around booster.

www.lazoo.org

BETTY WHITE TRIVIA: Betty's devotion to animals prompted her to pass on a role in James Brooks's 1997 Academy Award–winning comedy *As Good as It Gets*, starring Jack Nicholson and Helen Hunt. Of course, Betty knew Brooks from back in the day when he was one of the cocreators of *The Mary Tyler Moore Show*. He offered her the role of Carol, Helen Hunt's character's mother, but she turned it down because of one particular scene featuring a puppy being dropped down a laundry chute. Even though the puppy in the film landed safely on a pile of laundry, Betty was worried that people might see the scene and try it at home. "I said as long as that scene was in the film, I wouldn't do it," Betty recalled. Instead, the role of Carol (Helen Hunt's character's mother) went to Academy Award–nominated Shirley Knight.

Don't Give Up on Your Dreams

Growing up, everybody's favorite sitcom star always wanted to be a forest ranger (and a writer, and a singer, and a zookeeper!), but back then, only boys could be forest rangers. In 2010, her childhood wish came true when the U.S. Forest Service made her an honorary forest ranger. During the ceremony at the John F. Kennedy Center for Performing Arts, U.S. Forest Service Chief Tom Tidwell apologized that Betty didn't have the opportunity to join the Forest Service as a young woman. "Judging from your illustrious career, you would have made marvelous contributions to our agency and to the cause of conservation across the United States," said Tidwell. "Betty, you are a role model for little girls—for all of us—never to give up on our dreams." [Today's U.S. Forest Service is 38 percent female.] White received a great big (bear) hug from Smokey Bear and showed off her new official ranger's hat and badge before emphasizing the importance of protecting nature.

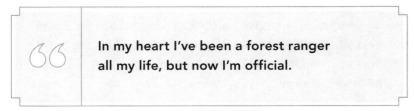

In my heart I've been a forest ranger all my life, but now I'm official.

CHAPTER FIVE

TRY NEW THINGS

LIKE THE REST OF AMERICA, WHITE WAS A fan of *The Mary Tyler Moore Show*, the hit sitcom that premiered on CBS in September 1970. But unlike the rest of the country, White had been following the sitcom's progress even before it went on the air. Allen Ludden and Grant Tinker, Mary Tyler Moore's then husband (and the cofounder, along with Moore, of MTM Productions), were old friends. Tinker and Moore formed a natural foursome with White and Ludden, and the two couples would frequently discuss the show's successes and challenges over dinner.

When the fourth season of the show was about to get underway, White received an unexpected Saturday morning phone call from Allan Burns, the cocreator of *The Mary Tyler Moore Show* (with Jim Brooks). Would she be interested in making a guest appearance on *The Mary Tyler Moore Show* the following week? The script called for someone "'as cloyingly sweet on the surface and something of a dragon underneath, with a tinge of nymphomania.' I was born for the role!" Betty later recalled.

She immediately said yes. Only later did she learn that the producers had been hesitant to cast her in the role of Sue Ann Nivens, even though the script called for someone "as sweet as Betty White but as vicious as a barracuda." It's funny to think of snarky Betty White as being described as simply "sweet," but back then, she was best known for the perky wife persona she had perfected on *Life with Elizabeth*. For years, she couldn't shake that "sickeningly sweet" image, even after saying "the bawdiest things" on game shows and talk shows. "The audience would think, 'Of course, poor sweet Betty doesn't know what she's saying. If only she knew what that really means,'" said White.

Her saccharine persona wasn't the issue when it came to casting, and nobody doubted that she would rock the role. The real concern was that if it didn't work out, things could get awkward between Betty and Mary, who were close friends. The producers tried out about ten actresses, but they still couldn't find someone sickeningly sweet enough for the part. Finally, according to White, the show's casting director said, "Just give the part to Betty. It's only a one-shot, and she's been around long enough that she won't hurt you."

In her first (and what was supposed to be only) appearance as Sue Ann Nivens, the relentlessly perky star of the fictional WJM-TV's "The Happy Homemaker" segment, White stole the show. Nauseatingly sugary and earnest on-air, Sue Ann delivers household tips in the most perky tone. As soon as the camera turns off, she "turns off" the "Happy

Homemaker" character and reverts to her usual conniving, backstabbing self.

The reaction to the two-faced, sexually voracious character was so overwhelmingly positive, that the show's producers told White right away that "she would no longer be just a one-night stand, so to speak," said White. The next morning when the doorbell rang, Betty opened the door to find Mary and Grant "grinning and holding some beautiful flowers." It seems they had come to tell Betty the good news in person. "Rotten Sue Ann would be coming back," Betty said. "The four of us had a very impromptu—and very festive—brunch."

Three weeks later, Sue Ann returned in another episode and "my career had been given a giant boost in the right direction," White said. Though Sue Ann was undeniably awful, White's nuanced performance helped us see she was also lonely and insecure . . . and hilarious! White had fun playing the "harpy." "She started out bad and then just got absolutely worse," she said of Sue Ann.

Sue Ann is deeply competitive and seems to relish pointing out her colleague's weaknesses, often in a passive-aggressive way (later in her career, you can see some Sue Ann in Elka on *Hot in Cleveland*). When she "congratulates" Mary on her promotion to a producer, it sounds more like an insult: "Mary, believe me. I'm proud that you haven't been disheartened by those who murmur that you've sacrificed your femininity to your ambition."

She exchanges barbs with newswriter Murray Slaughter, played by Gavin MacLeod, who often teases her about her promiscuity ("slut shaming" wasn't a thing back then). "Sue Ann, you'd have time to chase men if you were being embalmed in an hour," says Murray in one episode. When Lou isn't sure what to get Sue Ann for her birthday, Murray quips, "What do you get for the woman who's had everyone?"

And Sue Ann is always quick with the snappy retort or subtle put-down, usually involving a swipe at Murray's bald head, which she was constantly mocking (and patting!).

"When Betty came in, there was a whole new relationship for Murray and Sue Ann Nivens that really worked," said MacLeod in the PBS documentary *Betty White: First Lady of Television*. He recalled one particular episode where Sue Ann hires Murray as a "producer" on her show, mostly, it seems, as an excuse to humiliate him. It starts with her demand that he call her "Miss Nivens" and gets exponentially worse from there. To prepare for her wedding-themed show, Sue Ann insists on putting Murray in a wedding gown. Sue Ann "did everything in that show to emasculate him," said MacLeod. "The poor guy, it was one thing after another. [His anger] was building until the final scene, where they had a cake on the table. She did something, and he picked her up, put her on the cake, and she rode the cake right down to the floor. Only Betty could ride a cake the way she rode that cake, like she had a bucking bronco between her legs."

After a decade or so making a living on game-show appearances, the role rebooted White's acting career and earned her back-to-back supporting actress Emmy wins and a fourth Emmy nomination. "Sue Ann Nivens came around and changed the whole picture," said White.

> **With Sue Ann, I was able to show another side that was kind of fun and a little lecherous and a little mean.**

Sue Ann Nivens's Best Episodes

White so fully inhabited the role that even diehard *Mary Tyler Moore Show* fans have a hard time believing she didn't sashay into the WJM newsroom until season four! Even then, she appeared in about half of the episodes. In each of the remaining seasons, she appeared in only a handful of episodes. "But people still remember Sue Ann. She was such a mess! And such fun to play," said Betty.

Thanks to Betty White's hilariously two-faced performance, every appearance was unforgettable, but here are five of the best:

"The Lars Affair"
(SEASON 4, EPISODE 1)

This 1973 episode introduces White as backstabbing newsroom nymphomaniac Sue Ann Nivens. Belying her sweet-natured on-screen persona and adorable dimples as "The Happy Homemaker," Nivens shamelessly beds Lars, the never-seen husband of Mary's friend Phyllis Lindstrom (hilariously played by Cloris Leachman, with as much gusto as White). But it's her oversized reaction ("Oh, my poor *baby!*") to her crestfallen chocolate soufflé that really amps up the laughs. Mary threatens to expose Sue Ann's affair, which is "not a good image for the Happy Homemaker," and—what do you know?—Sue Ann chooses her career over her one-night stand. She doesn't want her nickname to be "The Happy Homewrecker." "I'm not doing it for myself, you see, but for all the ladies out there who *need* me," she insists. Sure, Sue Ann.

"A New Sue Ann"
(SEASON 5, EPISODE 7)

In a takeoff on *All About Eve*, Gloria Munson (Linda Kelsey, who later co-starred with Ed Asner on the MTM spinoff Lou Grant), a young fan, tries to steal Sue Ann's "Happy Homemaker" show out from under her by cozying up to the station manager. Mary asks why she's so worried about Gloria getting to be friendly with the station manager since it's no guarantee she'll get the job. "How do you think I got it?!" responds Sue Ann. She's shameless! The station manager ends up giving Gloria a baking segment on the show, to which Sue Ann responds snarkily: "Perhaps he has a weakness for tarts." To retaliate, Sue Ann frames Gloria for giving everyone in the station—including herself!—food poisoning from—what else, but—spoiled cream puffs!

"What Are Friends For?"
(SEASON 5, EPISODE 10)

When Sue Ann and Mary are in connecting hotel rooms at the broadcasters' convention in Chicago, Sue Ann is eager to show off her Chicago connections. After all, it's where she had her first cooking show, *Let's Talk About Meat*; but somehow, none of her old colleagues seem to care that she's in town. Mary wants a quiet night at the hotel room, but Sue Ann invites some conventioneers into Mary's room. Sue Ann, as usual, tries to be the life of the party, but all of the men they meet—including a convention of morticians—seem to prefer Mary's company. "Doesn't it ever bother you that you were the obvious favorite of a group of men who spend all their time with dead people?" Sue Ann snipes. But beneath her bitterness and spite, Sue Ann is just vulnerable and lonely, and she cries on Mary's shoulder. Instead of being pathetic, it's hilarious, as Sue Ann says, "You know what I hate most about crying? Your dimples don't show."

"Once I Had a Secret Love"
(SEASON 6, EPISODE 18)

Sue Ann finally beds Lou and—what a surprise—he's drunk at the time. Embarrassed and hung-over after their one-night stand, Lou skulks into the newsroom and tries to keep their affair a secret. He tells Sue Ann, "It's very important to me that no one knows what happened last night." "Oh, Lou, you silly," Sue Ann says brightly. "Everyone will know by the roses in your cheeks!" If they don't, Sue Ann will be sure to spread the word. "I didn't sleep a wink all night. I feel wonderful!" she announces to the newsroom before returning the socks that Lou left at her place. Later, Lou apologizes to Sue Ann and hopes he didn't "take advantage" of her. In perfect Sue Ann fashion, she compares their dalliance to food. "Lou, you were wonderful. If you were a soufflé, you would raise high in the pan! If you were a Crêpes Suzette, your flame would light a whole room!" Way to boost his ego, Sue Ann.

"Sue Ann's Sister"

Sue Ann becomes depressed and takes to her bed when her younger sister shows up in town with an offer to work on a competing homemaker show in Minneapolis. When the newsroom gang pays the bedridden Sue Ann a visit to cheer her up, they get a look at her over-the-top bedroom. Leave it to Sue Ann to have a frilly sexed-up boudoir, complete with a mirror on the ceiling and a huge vibrating round bed! "Did you decorate it yourself?" asks Murray. "Or did you have a sex maniac come in?"

On Friendship (and Famous Friends)

Even though Betty always found it easier to get along with animals than people, she managed to create many meaningful lifelong human bonds. Friendship takes work, and given White was a self-described workaholic, it makes sense that most of her friends were also in show business. Regardless of whether your friends are movie stars, Betty recognizes that "friendship takes time and energy if it's going to work." You've got to nurture a friendship—which is hard when you're busy being a show business goddess! Betty's advice: "Friendship can be so comfortable, but nurture it—don't take it for granted."

* Through her marriage to Allen, Betty developed a friendship with famed author **John Steinbeck** (*The Grapes of Wrath*, *Of Mice and Men*) and his third wife, Elaine. Allen had been friends with Elaine since they met at the University of Texas many years earlier. White admitted that it was "hard not to be a little in awe of John at first." It didn't help that the first time Betty was introduced to Steinbeck, he was in the middle of working on his acceptance speech for the Nobel Prize! He even asked Betty for suggestions. (He had been awarded the 1962 Nobel Prize in Literature.)

* Another old friend was comedian, producer, and director **Carl Reiner** (*The Dick Van Dyke Show*), who had served in the army with Allen in World War II. She first met Reiner when Allen invited all of "the guys from his outfit" to their house for a reunion. After Allen's death, they continued to be close friends. Reiner went on to play White's boyfriend Max on *Hot in Cleveland*!

* **Lucille Ball** of *I Love Lucy* fame became close friends with Betty from the time they first met in the 1950s while they were both working in the early days of TV. Betty's 1957 sitcom *A Date with the Angels* taped at Lucy's Desilu Studios. During a Reddit 2014 AMA forum, White said, "Lucy was one of my dearest friends. Our mothers were best friends. She was dynamite. Everything you saw was what you got."

* After working alongside **Rue McClanahan** on both *Mama's Family* and *The Golden Girls*, White and McClanahan became

close friends, often playing games between scenes on set. After *The Golden Girls* and its sequel *The Golden Palace* went off the air, White and McClanahan continued to have the closest relationship among the group over the years, until McClanahan's death in 2010.

* In an updated introduction to her book *In Person* in 2010, White wrote that losing all three of her costars including, "just recently, my beloved Rue McClanahan, has been very hard to take. When you work so closely together, for so long, and are blessed with such success, you wind up locked at the heart."

Take Disappointments in Stride

In its seventh season, *The Mary Tyler Moore Show* opted to end while it was a steady ratings performer (though not the hit it once was). Many of the cast members, including Valerie Harper and Cloris Leachman, had already left for spin-offs of their own, and Ed Asner was offered a one-year contract to do a weekly drama series based on his character, Lou Grant. Midway through the final season, "the powers that be" told Betty they'd like for her to get a spin-off of her own. Unfortunately, by that point, the MTM-produced spin-offs *Rhoda* and *Phyllis* were barely holding their own in the ratings department. Therefore, the producers decided they should build a whole new show for Betty rather than spin off the Sue Ann character.

"They thought she might be a little much to take every week, and if they knocked some of the edge off of her, they would destroy the character," Betty explained. Building an entirely new show from scratch is a difficult assignment under the best of circumstances, but it wouldn't be easy to convince the audience she wasn't playing the character they had come to love, Sue Ann Nivens.

The new series would center around a character named Joyce Whitman, a television actress who stars in her own police show, *Undercover Woman* (a takeoff on Angie Dickinson's show *Police Woman*). It would be Joyce's dream job except for the fact that her ex-husband is the director of the show-within-the-show. John Hillerman, who is best known for his work in later years on *Magnum, P.I.*, was cast as her ex-husband, the TV director. *The Mary Tyler Moore Show*'s Georgia Engel, who had played Georgette Baxter, was cast as Mitzi Maloney, Joyce's best friend.

What to call the show so that MTM fans would know Betty wasn't going to be playing Sue Ann? "We couldn't keep referring to our project as 'the show'; it had to have a title. *Sue Ann* was out; no one would know who *Joyce* was; so the working title stuck—*The Betty White Show*," Betty recalled. "Perhaps the fourth time would be the charm."

Alas, it was not to be.

The third televised iteration of *The Betty White Show* (and the fourth overall) premiered on CBS in September 1977, just six months after *The Mary Tyler Moore Show* aired its series finale on the network. The chemistry between Betty and her costars didn't quite work. Nonetheless, they soon developed a natural banter and enjoyed working with each other. Unfortunately, after fourteen shows (including the pilot), CBS opted not to pick the show up. The ratings had been okay, but the sitcom was no match opposite ABC's *Monday Night Football* and *The NBC Monday Movie*. Bob Daly, president of CBS, later acknowledged that he may have been a little hasty in canceling the show so quickly. But that was little comfort to Betty and her costars.

The cancellation of (yet another!) *The Betty White Show* was a surprise to Betty since the cast had just wrapped up its scheduled production with expectations to return to do future shows. She was disappointed, of course, but she knew that she was following the right path. Still, it was a bummer to have yet another *Betty White Show* get yanked off the air.

"There's sadness, but there's survival, too," White said after the show was cancelled in 1978. "You have to walk on. I wouldn't leave this business for anything in the world. It's the only game there is for me."

Betty is the rare performer who's been on three hit series, but that doesn't mean her career hasn't had its fair shares of setbacks and disappointments. Everyone has failures. It's all about how you handle those failures and what comes next. Betty's response to disappointment was to keep busy with work.

From the late 1970s to the early to mid-1980s, she rarely had a break in the action. In addition to starring in TV movies and appearing on a variety of sitcoms, she joined the antics on *The Carol Burnett Show* and had a recurring role in its spin-off, *Mama's Family,* in 1983 and 1984, where she worked alongside her future *Golden Girls* costar Rue McClanahan. "From the first time I guested on the show [*The Carol Burnett Show*], I was tickled to be included in those sketches as Eunice's (Carol Burnett's) spoiled, rich, bitchy sister, Ellen. Mean as she was, Ellen was the apple of Mama's eye and took credit for whatever poor Eunice had knocked herself out to do," said Betty.

Cruising on *The Love Boat* gave White a chance to reconnect with her former *Mary Tyler Moore* foil, Gavin MacLeod, who went from Murray to playing Captain Stubing. In her memoir, *If You Ask Me (And of Course You Won't)*, White confessed that "it was so hard not to stroke that bald head!" White appeared on the star-studded series a number of times, primarily as the character of Betsy Boucher, who comes on the cruise with her friend Sylvia Duvall, played by none other than White's real-life gal pal, Broadway legend Carol Channing. In the 1982 episode "My Friend, the Executrix," the two showbiz veterans put on a barbershop-type song-and-dance number and impress the cruise passengers (they were impressed!). White's favorite appearance on the show was probably a 1980 episode in which she plays opposite her off-screen husband, Allen Ludden, just a year before he passed away of stomach cancer.

It's easy now to look back at Betty's career and focus on the amazing string of hits she had, but she also had a fair share of professional setbacks and moments when she worried she might never work again. Just because one show is cancelled or your pilot isn't picked up, you feel like you'll never get another job again. But that's not the case. Betty's weathered the dramatic ups and downs of her career by keeping an even keel and staying busy rather than wallowing! She's a good reminder that you're never too old for a second or third or fourth act.

66 **I get bored with people who complain about this or that. It's such a waste of time.**

Betty White by the Numbers

* Year in which she began her TV career on an "experimental" broadcast in LA: **1939**

* Year in which she first appeared on *Password*: **1961**

* Number of times in which she appeared on the original *Password*: **44**

* Number of times hosting Tournament of Roses Parade: **19**

* Year in which she was inducted into the Television Hall of Fame: **1995**

* Number of credits on IMDb for Betty White playing herself: **349**

* Year in which she received her first and only Grammy: **2012**

* Number of decades in which Betty has worked in the entertainment business: **8**

* Number of times in which she's played herself on *The Simpsons*: **2**

* Age at which she hosted *Saturday Night Live* for the first time: **88**

* Age at which she executive produced *Betty White's Off Their Rockers*: **90**

* Age at which she provided the voice of Bitey White in *Toy Story 4*: **97**

* Number of followers on Twitter (as of press time): **1.5 million**

CHAPTER SIX

THANK YOU FOR BEING A FRIEND

SHE'S A PAL AND A CONFIDANTE! ONE OF the reasons Betty continues to work regularly is that her colleagues love having her around. Her career serves as a good reminder that you never know what opportunity might fall in your lap—well, especially if you're a perky, all-American quipster. The versatile performer was working on *The Carol Burnett* spin-off, *Mama's Family,* and making assorted guest appearances when she got word that the A-list TV production company Witt/Thomas/Harris, the team behind successful prime-time shows like *Soap* and *It's a Living* was putting a new show together. Aware of the producers' track record and reputation, White was immediately intrigued. What really piqued her interest was the fact that Jay Sandrich, a regular

Mary Tyler Moore Show director, had signed on to direct the pilot for the new show, which would be called *The Golden Girls.*

Once she read the pilot script for *The Golden Girls,* "I really started to sit up and pay attention," White said. "The premise—four older women living together in Miami—hadn't sounded particularly attractive, but the script came alive with some of the best writing I'd seen since *MTM.*"

After her successful run as the hypersexual Sue Ann Nivens, White naturally assumed she would play Blanche, who was equally man-hungry. She learned that Bea Arthur (best known as the title character on *Maude*) would be playing Dorothy, the snarky Brooklynite, and Broadway star Estelle Getty had been signed on to play Dorothy's mother, Sophia. "It was assumed that I would be Blanche, the well-to-do Southern woman to whom men were the breath of life. The fourth character was Rose, and they had settled on Rue McClanahan." McClanahan had most recently played a shy, mousy character on *Mama's Family.*

"The next report I heard was a call saying a decision had been made to switch parts. I would be playing Rose, and Rue would do Blanche." Initially, Betty was disappointed since playing another character like the naughty Nivens sounded like fun. Sandrich had a different reaction. "If Betty plays another nymphomaniac, they are going to think it is Sue Ann Nivens all over again," he said. Once she understood Sandrich's rationale, White came to realize it was a brilliant idea. "It suddenly made perfect sense—not just because I loved Jay, but because he was absolutely right."

Sandrich also provided the insight into the character of Rose that she needed. "She is not dumb—just totally naive," he told her. "She believes everything she is told and, in her innocence, always takes the first meaning of every word." Rose took everything literally and didn't understand sarcasm, but she "was not weak. She had her own set of rules that made perfect sense, if only to her, and she also had a fierce Nordic temper on occasion," said White.

White never regretted taking the Rose role, and she commended McClanahan on her performance, saying she "took Blanche and ran with her—farther than I would ever have dared to go. She was wonderfully outrageous and outrageously wonderful." McClanahan was equally complimentary about White's take on Rose. "Betty was hysterical as Rose."

BETTY WHITE TRIVIA: Rue had worked with Bea for five and a half years on *Maude*, and Betty and Rue worked together for a couple of years on *Mama's Family*.

Now that they had assembled the perfect cast, the question was: Would viewers tune in to watch a show about women who were of, shall we say, a certain age? Like the Ice Age? Let's face it, folks, these gals weren't pin-up models like the babes on *Charlie's Angels*, which had gone off the air just a few years before *The Golden Girls* launched (and prompted one NBC executive to coin the phrase "Jiggle TV," to refer to the trend toward scantily clad blondes without bras dominating prime time in the late 1970s). Would great writing, a cast of show business pros, and brilliant comic acting be enough of a draw? On a Saturday night? That was traditionally not a great time slot (though *The Mary Tyler Moore Show* found success there).

The answer came on September 14, 1985, when *The Golden Girls* premiered and was an instant hit. The *Los Angeles Times* proclaimed the show "the best new comedy of the season." It was also the most watched program of the week, attracting viewers in 21.5 million homes on Saturday night, eclipsing NBC's biggest hit at the time, *The Cosby Show*. It scored the highest premiere ratings for any NBC comedy since the 1974 debut of *Chico and the Man*. Of course, in those pre-Internet, early cable TV days, there wasn't nearly as much competition for viewership. For perspective, NBC considered its workplace sitcom *Superstore* a relative hit in 2019, when it attracted 3.8 million viewers. (Of course, our population has grown, which skews those numbers, but you get the general idea.)

What was perhaps most impressive—and surprising—was the way *The Golden Girls* crossed all the demographic lines. The show seemed to appeal to a cross-section of America, particularly in terms of age. "How was our show able to reach all the age groups? Perhaps because we weren't specifically aiming at any one of them, but mainly, I think, because we were truly funny," Betty said.

And so it was that at age sixty-three, Betty White would become a TV star yet again, this time in one of the most memorable roles of her career: the sweet, dim-witted Minnesotan, Rose Nylund.

> I fell in love with her. I loved Rose. Rose didn't have a mean bone in her body.

In playing the part of Rose, White never forgot Sandrich's clue to the character: "Rose couldn't ever look like she got it. She had to be innocence personified." She takes things so literally that when Sophia says you can get pregnant in Sicily just by crossing the street, Rose believes her. The girls are constantly telling Rose to shut up—and sometimes it's for a good reason. When Dorothy teases Rose about her idyllic childhood, Rose gets serious: She had her "fair share of troubles" in St. Olaf, like the time "a mysterious drifter stole our butter churn."

Getting laughs out of these lines seems effortless, but it's not. Betty, like all masters of their craft, just makes it seem that way. In her expert hands, Rose isn't a simple-minded character, but an endearing one. Her pop-eyed pantomime as she delivers a zinger lets you laugh at her and with her at the same time. And when she delivers, she waits for the laugh, and she knows how long to wait. Fortunately, the show's writers gave her some great one-liners to work with: "I had an imaginary friend, but he'd never tell me his name," she says in one episode. Most of Rose's jokes are long, shaggy-dog-in-St.-Olaf-type stories that never seem to relate to what's going on around her, though you know in her head, it probably makes perfect sense.

She always has an old Scandinavian saying for any occasion, and they're generally indecipherable. For example: "You can let two angry mackerel fight it out in a purse, but don't ever plan on carrying that purse to a formal affair." Even Rose has to admit, it may have lost something in translation! Then there are all of the times when she breaks out anecdotes from her childhood on the farm in St. Olaf.

Whatever meandering tale she's telling us, we almost never get to hear the end of it—the girls tell her to shut up first. But as Rose clams up, we can see from her face that she's finishing that joke in her head. When Blanche asks the girls if they've ever had a man refuse to sleep with them, Rose promises she's got a "story that will end all stories" and the girls instantly moan. "Oh, Rose!" Blanche tells her, "Honey, make it fast, ten words or less, just spit it out. When was it that a man refused to sleep with you?" She gets a distant, spacy look in her eyes and says plainly, "The time I was radioactive." The girls get back to their conversation, and we never hear the whole story! Her life story is an ancient scroll, a partially deciphered manuscript, half-lost in the shifting snow of St. Olaf.

When the girls visit a psychiatrist to work through their "issues," Dorothy tells him how Rose is so stupid that she mistakenly placed a classified ad "Willing to do anything, eight dollars per hour" in the personals and was surprised when a whole bunch of guys responded. Blanche says, "The point is, Rose, you're doing something stupid all of the time. And if you're not doing something stupid, or saying something stupid, or wearing something stupid, you're cooking something stupid." This is too much! Rose finally shows her thorns. She calls Blanche one of her favorite Swedish insults—a "gerchominochen," which roughly translates to the precise moment that dog poop turns white (Ewww!).

Our sweet Rose can be surprisingly bitchy—there's a little bit of a nod to Sue Ann Nivens as well as an inkling of the future Elka on *Hot in Cleveland* in her character. For instance, like Sue Ann, Rose is fiercely competitive; take the episode where she dumps Blanche for Dorothy in a bowling competition. "Dorothy's a better bowler than you and I want to win this year," she says. Athletics turn Rose from a lamb into a wolf. "I've never told anybody this, but I had to transfer high schools because of a field hockey incident," she explains.

Both sweet and saucy, Rose's character is developed through the series by events that are sometimes pleasant and sometimes not. We see our flower endure through all sorts of physical and psychological hardships, always with grace. When their Miami house is robbed, Rose buys a gun. She's so afraid, she won't eat or sleep. In season two, she has an esophageal spasm that has Rose convinced that she temporarily died and went to Heaven. In season six, Rose finally reveals that she's addicted to painkillers due to an old farming injury. She goes to rehab and the issue is never raised again. Gotta love the magic of TV! In the final season, Rose suffers a major heart attack and has to have a triple bypass surgery. In another episode, she's sexually assaulted by her dentist! But through it all, she's still naive, optimistic, kindhearted Rose.

"The glass is always half full as far as Rose is concerned," Betty said of the character. "Life is a musical comedy as far as she's concerned. It's always going to have a happy ending." The same could be said of Betty White!

The Golden Girls is a unicorn of a sitcom—that rare instance where a show is an instant hit and stays that way throughout most of its run (it remained in the top ten for its first five seasons before moving time slots). More than 27 million people tuned in for the hour-long series finale on May 9, 1992, an impressive number (ranking in the top 20 most watched TV series finales of all time). Unlike the vast majority of sitcoms, *The Golden Girls* ended on its own terms rather than because it was yanked off the schedule. At least that was part of the story.

The other part is that Bea Arthur was ready to retire from prime time. There was no way they would be able to do *The Golden Girls* without her (nor would they want to). *Golden Girls* creator Susan Harris came up with a great idea that would enable the gang to stay together in a spin-off starring White, McClanahan, and the rest of the gang. After Dorothy (Bea Arthur) marries Blanche's uncle in the series finale of *The Golden Girls*, the other roomies sell the house and buy an Art Deco Miami hotel. Initially, the three stars were skeptical about jumping into a new show right away, but Harris was persuasive.

> The old saying about one door closes and another opens is true. There have been times when a show has ended, and I've thought that's the end of the world. But after that, something else comes along.

The new show would be called *The Golden Palace*, a reference to the name of the new hotel. Another big change: Rather than airing on NBC like *The Golden Girls*, the spin-off would air on CBS (NBC had declined to guarantee the new show a full-season commitment). Maybe it would signal a new start. Perhaps to compensate for Arthur's absence, the producers introduced new characters played by newcomer Don Cheadle as the hotel manager and Cheech Marin, of Cheech and Chong fame, as the hotel's chef.

Although Arthur showed up on the series twice as now-remarried Dorothy, the chemistry was off. The series wasn't a disaster, but it also never fell into a groove. Without Arthur, something was missing. There were other guest stars including Betty's old costars Tim Conway, Harvey Korman, and Eddie Albert, as well as veteran comedian George Burns and then up-and-coming comics like Margaret Cho, Bobcat Goldthwait, Carol Leifer, and Jack Black, who played a taxi driver in one episode. Unfortunately, a great lineup of talent didn't help the show take off in the ratings.

As Betty later wrote, "The show was enjoyable, the reviewers were kind, and the ratings were satisfactory. In other words, *The Golden Palace* was a moderately pleasing show—not a grabber." It was not renewed for a second season, a disappointment but not a total surprise. Betty had been around the block enough by this point to understand that a life in show business (or just in general) involved a lot of highs and lows. She knew how to ride out the lows by focusing on the highs (and staying busy!).

> A wisecracking substitute schoolteacher, an oversexed egomaniac, and a feisty old lady who had a mouth like a sailor.

The Golden Girls and the Gay Fans Who Love Them

In *The Q Guide to The Golden Girls*, author Jim Colucci writes about the strong connection between the LGBTQ+ community and the show. For many in the LGBTQ+ community, the sitcom expanded the definition of family. As *Golden Girls* creator Susan Harris told *Out* magazine, the series "showed that you didn't need the customary, traditional relationship to be happy. It paints a picture of all of the possibilities for family."

The show's grandmotherly stars model acceptance. Sure, at first Blanche wasn't thrilled about her brother Clayton being gay. She said stupid things like: "I don't really mind Clayton being homosexual. I just don't like him dating men." But her friends set her straight, so to speak. Why shouldn't Blanche's brother marry the man he loves? Given that gay marriage was still decades away, the episode "Sister of the Bride," in which Clayton marries his partner, Doug, is ahead of its time. If Blanche can reckon with her homophobia, viewers at home were challenged to do the same.

Then there's the time that Dorothy's college friend Jean (Lois Nettleton), a lesbian, falls for Rose, who mistakes the word "lesbian" for "Lebanese." Haha! Though Rose doesn't reciprocate Jean's feelings, she doesn't make a huge fuss out of it, and she embraces Jean as a friend—sending a clear message to the audience that having a gay friend is no big deal! If it's okay with Rose, it must be okay.

In episode five, Rose has an HIV scare when she learns that a blood transfusion she received may have been tainted. For 1990, the episode "72 Hours" was daring since few TV shows—especially sitcoms—even made mention of the AIDS crisis at the time. Anxiously awaiting the results of her test (that's the 72 hours in the episode's title), Rose asks Blanche, "Why is this happening to me? I mean, this shouldn't happen to people like me." To which Blanche replies, "AIDS is not a bad person's disease, Rose. It is not God punishing people for their sins." Once again, the show was trying to educate their audience not by lecturing but by modeling compassionate behavior.

Years later, Betty explained why it was a bold choice for the producers to place Rose, of all the characters, in this predicament. "Not only were people understandably afraid of AIDS, but a lot of people wouldn't even admit it existed," White told Colucci. "So this was a daring episode to do, and the writers went straight for it. It's interesting that they picked Rose for that situation. Blanche was such a busy lady, but if it had been her story, it would have taken on a whole other color. But with Rose being Miss Not-Always-With-It, it came as a real surprise."

Off-screen, White was always a proponent of gay rights. Her close friends over the years included (then closeted) gay stars such as Liberace, Rock Hudson, and Merv Griffin. In fact, she would often attend premieres with Liberace (who she called Lee) early in her career. In the summer of 1985, Betty made sure to get her friend Rock Hudson, who had recently gone public with his AIDS diagnosis, advance copies of the first few episodes of *The Golden Girls*. Betty told Colucci that she had a sense that he would love it—and he did. The film star and friend died just a couple of months later.

When asked how she feels about her gay fans, Betty told Larry King, "I don't care whom you sleep with. It's what kind of a human being are you? I don't understand. It's such a personal private business and none of mine." She got a kick out of the fact that on Saturday nights when *The Golden Girls* was on at 9 p.m., gay bars would turn down the music so the crowd could watch their favorite show. "Then, at 9:30, they'd turn it off and start the dancing again. We felt very honored," she told the Paley Center audience in 2006.

Over the years, there have been any number of *Golden Girls* spoof productions and tributes in the gay community. In 2003, four gay male friends created an all-drag stage show version of the sitcom called "Golden Girls . . . Live." [Unfortunately, they hit some issues with rights and the production was short-lived.] But there would be many more drag tributes to come!

Betty wasn't surprised at her queer appeal. "Throughout my career, I've always portrayed characters that were humorous but also weren't afraid to speak their minds, especially when it came to racy or controversial topics," she said in a 2011 interview. "I think this struck a chord with the LGBT community."

Golden Girls and Controversy

Yes, over the course of its seven-season run, the hit sitcom boldly tackled issues that most prime-time sitcoms avoid: addiction, sexual harassment, same-sex marriage, and the HIV/AIDS crisis. But that doesn't mean they handled these topics in the same way we would today. We can be wild about *The Golden Girls* while also acknowledging that the characters' take on race, gender, sexuality, and so much else is outdated and in some cases downright offensive. Attitudes about these issues have changed since the late 1980s and early 1990s, when the show first aired. In 2020, amid the backdrop of Black Lives Matter protests, Hulu removed an episode of the sitcom due to concerns over blackface.

The 1988 episode of the sitcom titled "Mixed Blessing" shows Dorothy's son, Michael (Scott Jacoby), planning to marry an older black woman, Lorraine (Rosalind Cash). In the episode, Blanche (Rue McClanahan) and Rose (Betty White) are wearing mud masks when they open the door to greet Michael's fiancée and her family.

"This is mud on our faces," White says in all earnestness. "We're not really black."

Hulu decided to pull the episode. To some, the decision was more of a symbolic act that gets muddled in the context of the series, which was far from "woke." Dr. Steven W. Thrasher pointed out in *New York* magazine, the "blackface" scene "might be one of the least racist things about the show." Thrasher detailed a number of flagrant examples of racism. "All four of the girls were racist," Thrasher wrote. "Rose once whooped it up in a Native American headdress and pretended to be an exchange student named Kim-Fung Toi, using a racist accent." So what's all the fuss about a face mask?

Back in St. Olaf . . .

Though St. Olaf isn't a real town in Minnesota, Rose brings her fictional hometown to life with her colorful and mostly unbelievable anecdotes.

Remember this is the town where Rose was voted "most likely to get stuck in a tuba" in high school and was also the valedictorian!

St. Olaf's biggest claim to fame (aside from the low IQ of its citizens) is its giant black hole, where townspeople could often be found on weekends "just standing around looking at it." This naturally prompts Dorothy to refer to St. Olaf sarcastically as the real "entertainment capital of the world." Another attraction that sets St. Olaf apart is Mt. Losenbauden, similar to Mount Rushmore, except that it features only the faces of losing presidential candidates. St. Olaf's famous trysting spot is called Mt. Pushover.

St. Olaf holidays and festivals include Hay Day (when the townsfolk celebrate hay), the Festival of the Dancing Sturgeons, the Day of the Wheat, and, of course, the Butter Queen competition.

Usually, Rose offers her stories as a lesson or to make a helpful point, but often they are completely unrelated to what the girls are talking about. As the series goes on, her anecdotes become more absurd, though they usually head in unexpected directions. There's the story about Ernest T. Minkie, St. Olaf's librarian who was also the town's only dentist. "Everybody hated Minkie; he seemed to take great pleasure in giving other people pain. They hated him so much that nobody ever went to the dentist or the library."

Her vivid—and offbeat—reminiscences about growing up in St. Olaf sometimes sounded more like the "plot" of a Fellini film. "When I think of my father, I always picture him pulling a giant tuna up Main Street. It wasn't a real tuna; it was made of chrysanthemums!" Then there was her biology teacher, Mrs. Gunderson, who taught students that the human body was made up of 80 percent Ovaltine. "During a course on World War I, she told us mustard gas was something you got from eating too many hot dogs," Rose recalls. "That's why, to this day in St. Olaf, everyone celebrates the Fourth of July with a thin omelet on a bun."

Rose likes to make Scandinavian desserts such as Genügenflürgen cake, which inevitably, leads to humorous interactions like the following:

Rose: It's an ancient recipe, but I Americanized it.

Dorothy: So one might say you brought "Genügenflürgen" into the '80s?

Rose: Yes, but I'm not one to blow my own Genügenflürgen.

Sophia: I can't even reach mine!

Classic Rose-isms

Not only does Rose trot out a St. Olaf story on just about any occasion, but she also consistently surprises the girls with her "off-beat perspective" on the world. Here are just a few of Rose's memorable, hilarious lines:

✳ "You know what they say: You can lead a herring to water, but you have to walk really fast or he'll die."

✳ "Sometimes people need help making decisions; that's the way it was with Thor, our pet lamb."

✳ "Could we get in trouble having a garage sale? I mean, after all, we're not actually selling a garage!"

* "I never had PMS. But I did have a BMW one time."

* "Am I the only one here who feels like taking off all her clothes and doing the hokey pokey?"

* "Doctors don't know everything, Dorothy. They think they do, but they don't. I mean after all, Dr. Seuss was a doctor, too."

Betty White Fashion Plate

As a young ingenue at the dawn of broadcasting, the fresh-faced brunette may not have been glamorous enough for Hollywood, but she brought a touch of Hollywood glamour to TV.

On *Life with Elizabeth*, she was a chic 1950s housewife in a fitted A-line dress, cinched with a classic black belt, and a scarf styled around her neck or maybe a string of pearls. And high heels! Because who doesn't cook and clean in high heels? In a press photo taken in 1954, Betty smiles confidently in a fitted forest green collared blouse with a gray A-line skirt and a bulky, colorful jewel necklace. With her hourglass figure, she's a classic '50s glamour girl.

In a photo shoot to promote *The Betty White Show* in 1958, Betty looks the vision of style and class in a fitted dress with white gloves, a hat with a veil, and a modern-looking translucent handbag! As she captivated the game-show, talk-show, and variety-show circuit throughout the 1960s, Betty adopted her signature bouffant hairstyle and bright red lipstick. She wouldn't go blonde until the following decade when she took on the role of Sue Ann Nivens for *The Mary Tyler Moore Show*.

Sue Ann knew how to emphasize her figure in feminine wrap-around dresses and solid-colored turtlenecks.

As Rose, the naive country girl from Minnesota on *The Golden Girls*, she dresses in feminine, romantic pastel combos—often a belted, buttoned, collared dress layered with a colorful cardigan or an oversized blazer. And she knows how to accessorize, with scarves, bangles, or oversized stud earrings. Even when she meets the gals in the kitchen for a midnight snack, Rose looks put together in her silky nightwear. Her look was always warm and homey—just like the character. In the 2020s, '80s fashion looks and "grandma" style became trendy, proving that everything old is new again if you wait long enough.

In 2020, InStyle.com went so far as to declare *The Golden Girls* a fashion inspiration, saying the girls are "just as well-dressed as the characters from *Sex and the City* or *Gossip Girl*." They may even qualify as "the best-dressed characters in TV history," with Rose getting points for her "ability to pull off any color combination." Now that certainly is a magical skill!

On *Hot in Cleveland*, Elka dresses in pastel tracksuits, which she bedazzles to make them snazzier. Animal lover that she is, Elka tends toward animal print clothing. The same was true of Betty as she grew older. In 2010, in an appearance on *Today*, she wore a black-and-white jacket and scarf featuring images of leopards and giraffes. Sounds gaudy, but on Betty, it looked magnificent.

Off-screen, Betty was always a fashion icon, and her personal style grew more distinctive and appreciated as she got older. In 2020, *Us Weekly* ran a story about "14 Times Betty White's Fashion Choices Were Hot as Hell." They highlighted the black gown with a mesh chest and sleeves that she wore to the 2nd Annual Comedy Awards in 1988, calling it "flashy but classy," which might be the best description of her style over the years. At the 42nd Annual Emmy Awards in 1990, White wowed in a long-sleeve champagne-colored gown with sequin embellishments. Couldn't get more flashy/classy than that!

BETTY WHITE TRIVIA: Including *The Golden Girls*, Betty played the character of Rose Nylund four times on four different TV series (all created by Susan Harris). She was a regular on the short-lived *Golden Girls* spin-off *The Golden Palace* (1992–93) and also popped up a few times on the more successful, long-running *Golden Girls* spin-off *Empty Nest* (1988, 1992) as well as on one episode of *Nurses*, the *Empty Nest* spin-off (1991). Then there was the time where she played a Washington bureaucrat on *St. Elsewhere* in 1985, and a psychiatric patient mistakes her for Sue Ann, the Happy Homemaker! "You must have me confused with somebody else," says White's character.

Are You a Sue Ann Nivens or a Rose Nylund?

1. In your free time, would you rather:
   a. Whip up your famous beef stroganoff
   b. Volunteer at the local homeless shelter
   c. Go to bars to hit on men
   d. Rescue a stray cat

2. People describe you as:
   a. Ambitious
   b. A little spacey
   c. Man-crazy
   d. Kind

3. Friends sometimes call you out for being:
   a. Too much of a pushover
   b. Too pushy
   c. Gullible
   d. Dramatic

4. You're never fully dressed without a:
   a. Smile
   b. Date
   c. Friend
   d. Pastel pantsuit

5. Your ideal job is:
   a. On-air personality
   b. Professional chef
   c. Counselor
   d. Dog walker

6. When a friend hurts your feelings, you:
   a. Get back at them by doing something spiteful
   b. Talk things through with them
   c. Bad-mouth them to coworkers
   d. Let it go. They were probably having a rough day!

7. You would describe your style as:
   a. Sexy
   b. Tracksuit casual
   c. Miami Beach retiree
   d. Sophisticated professional

8. If someone wants your opinion, you:
   a. Give it to them straight
   b. Beat around the bush
   c. Tell them what you think they want to hear
   d. Try to give it to them gently

9. You'd like to be remembered for:
   a. Being kind
   b. Being famous
   c. Being rich
   d. Being generous

10. You love to talk about:

   a. Animals

   b. Your hometown

   c. Your latest culinary adventure

   d. Yourself

Add up your responses.

If more than five of your answers were "Sue Ann," then you're more like Sue Ann Nivens!

Okay, let's be honest. You might be a little bit pushy, but that's only because you care. You love to cook—and you love to talk about yourself even more. Sure, you've always got sex on the brain, but what's wrong with that? You're fabulous and you know it!

If more than five of your answers were "Rose Nylund," then you're more like Rose Nylund!

Your heart is true. You see the best of people and want the best for them, too. Sure, sometimes you can be a little naive or a little slow, but you mean well. You're a kind-hearted optimist, an animal lover, and a good friend!

CHAPTER SEVEN

USE IT OR LOSE IT

ONE OF THE MANY REASONS WE LOVE

Betty White is because she appreciates every opportunity that comes her way. After seven golden seasons on *The Golden Girls* and one season on *The Golden Palace*, White was more in demand than ever, and she certainly wasn't ready to slow down. Unlike some performers who hold out for the perfect role, she was never precious about the parts she accepted. There was no such thing as a "small part" to her, and her inner glow shined through every character. She was happy to have the work, and her midwestern work ethic served her well, showing up on time with her lines memorized.

She loved to perform and was never one to snub her nose at soap operas, game shows, talk shows, movies of the week, and other opportunities that came her way over the years. What's the point in having all of that talent and charm if you don't put it to use? And use it she did in a steady stream of performances. Credited in more than 115 acting titles (not including the hundreds of times she appeared as "herself" on game shows, variety, etc.), spanning from the early 1950s to 2020, Betty is the rare actor with no gaps in her résumé—for eight decades! Below are just some of her most memorable TV performances from the early '90s to the late aughts (when she became even hotter!):

Bob (1993)

Betty joined the cast of the second season of the reworked Bob Newhart vehicle as Sylvia Schmidt, who runs a greeting card company that employs Bob (formerly a comic in season one). The two TV legends had never worked together before but had first met years earlier when they were both frequent guests on *The Jack Paar Show*. On the character of Schmidt, White told the *Los Angeles Times* when she joined the show's cast: "She's not Sue Ann Nivens and she's not Rose Nyland, either. She's much more sophisticated than Rose, which is not tough (laughing). And she's not the neighborhood nymphomaniac or the witch that Sue Ann was." Unfortunately, CBS didn't give the revamped *Bob* much time to get into a groove before pulling it off the air after only six episodes. In addition to Betty's performance, there's another reason *Bob* was noteworthy: It featured a then unknown young actress named Lisa Kudrow, who was cast in her iconic role of Phoebe Buffay on the sitcom *Friends* soon after *Bob* was scrapped. In 2015, Betty and Bob got to work together again, this time on her show *Hot in Cleveland*. In fact, in the series finale, they marry!

Maybe This Time (1995–96)

This ABC sitcom only lasted one season, but during that time, Betty had a blast playing Shirley Wallace, a five-times-married man-crazy Sue Ann Nivens–type flirt. Another plus for Betty was the opportunity to work alongside Marie Osmond, who played Julia, her character's recently divorced daughter. This show is also noteworthy because it brought Craig Ferguson to the United States from his native Scotland. After the series ended, ABC added Ferguson to the cast of *The Drew Carey Show* as Carey's boss. Ferguson and White struck up a long-lasting friendship, and she regularly appeared on CBS's *The Late Late Show with Craig Ferguson* during its decade-long run. "He's just incredible," Betty said in 2010. "We can't dare make eye contact because we'll both crack up. We just tickle each other."

The John Larroquette Show (1996)

Just a little less than four years after *The Golden Girls* wrapped its run, Betty White, Rue McClanahan, and Estelle Getty reunited on NBC's *The John Larroquette Show*. In an episode titled "Here We Go Again," in reference to Betty's then recently published memoir of the same name, Betty plays a parody of herself. The show's satire of *Sunset Boulevard* features Betty as "the Norma Desmond of TV" who has penned *Golden Girls: The Musical* and coerces Larroquette (Debra Jo Rupp) into polishing it. As in the movie it's spoofing, this episode has Betty acting the diva and making the moves on John, who eventually ends up facedown in a swimming pool. McClanahan and Getty show up to join the fun as themselves. Along with Larroquette in drag as Bea Arthur, they perform "Golden Girls: The Musical." Talk about meta! The episode earned White yet another Emmy Award, this time for Outstanding Guest Actress in a Comedy Series.

> **FUN FACT:** *The John Larroquette Show* was produced by the same team behind *The Golden Girls*. Also, White and Larroquette later reunited on *Boston Legal* (see below).

Ally McBeal (1999)

In one memorable episode, Betty played Ally McBeal's (Calista Flockhart) therapist, the pill-pushing Dr. Shirley Flott, who confesses to a fondness for suppositories. When Ally is reluctant to try Prozac, Dr. Flott tells her, "I've been a therapist since before you were born, so you're going to have to trust me when I tell you that you won't find happiness through love or by turning to God. It comes in a pill. There can even be joy in the taking. Mine comes in suppository form. Gives me a little wriggle." She then does a little wriggle (with a giggle).

Ladies Man (1999–2001)

Betty costarred in the CBS sitcom as Mitzi Stiles, the mother of Jimmy Stiles (Alfred Molina), a furniture maker juggling the many women in his life (including his daughter, played by future *Big Bang Theory* star, Kaley Cuoco). The season one finale featured Betty's former *Golden Girls* costars Rue McClanahan and Estelle Getty in what turned into a mini–*Golden Girls* reunion (alas, no Bea Arthur). The episode marked the last time White, Getty, and McClanahan acted together.

Suddenly Susan (1996)

In an episode entitled "Golden Girl Friday," Betty plays Midge Haber, a seemingly sweet senior citizen, who is actually a con artist who sues for age discrimination. This appearance earned Betty an Emmy nomination for Guest Actress in a Comedy series.

That '70s Show (2002–03)

Betty played Bea Sigurdson, Kitty Forman's (Debra Jo Rupp) sweet-seeming, acid-tongued mother, a riff on her *MTM* character Sue Ann Nivens and a precursor to Elka Ostrovsky on *Hot in Cleveland*. She appeared in four episodes before vanishing never to be seen again. But we haven't forgotten her!

The Bold and the Beautiful (2006–09)

Betty was always bold *and* beautiful, so it made perfect sense to appear on the award-winning daytime drama (which was spun off from *The Young and the Restless*). As Ann Douglas, estranged mother to longtime character Stephanie Forrester (Susan Flannery), Betty first appeared in an episode where Stephanie confronts her about childhood abuse. The story line ended twenty-three episodes and three years later with Ann's death. "We did the shoot on Paradise Cove at Malibu, and as she walked off the dock and into the blue beyond and died, it really was dying with dignity," the show's executive producer and head writer Bradley Phillip Bell said. "She was unplugged from the machines. Her daughters had kidnapped her from the hospital and brought her to a beautiful place, and she passed in a very beautiful way. It was incredible." Of course, it was!

Boston Legal (2005–08)

From 2005 to 2008, White had a blast chewing up the scenery on ABC's *Boston Legal* as the duplicitous, blackmailing secretary Catherine Piper, a role she had originated as a guest star on *Boston Legal*'s precursor, *The Practice*, in 2004 (and earned her yet another Emmy nomination!). Though she might look like a sweet old lady, the nefarious Piper, who appeared on thirty episodes of the juicy law drama, was responsible for a murder and multiple armed robberies.

Ugly Betty (2007)

In a guest shot as herself during season two of the ABC dramedy, Betty gets her hand slammed in a cab door. The culprit is none other than diva-ish villain Wilhelmina Slater (Vanessa Williams), who's been trying to repair her nasty image. Betty plays up her over-the-top bitchy persona. "Oh my God! It's Betty White," exclaims a man with his boyfriend when they spot her on the sidewalk holding her bloody hand. "Yes, it's Betty White, jackass. I'm on the ground here. Call 911!" They call 911, but not before taking a selfie with the star.

The incident goes viral, and Wilhelmina is eager to repair her public image. She visits Betty in the hospital, bringing along the news cameras. Betty, in a hospital bed, recoils from Wilhelmina and acts like she's in agony. "Get the monster away from me!" She totally hams it up until Wilhelmina orders the cameras to stop. "Have you lost your mind, old lady?" Wilhelmina asks.

Not at all. Just the opposite. "I'm gonna milk it 'til it's dry," she tells Wilhelmina, poking fun at Betty's sudden burst of fame. She needs the money because "that *Golden Girls* money went right into the nickel slots!"

Picture her, parked on a chair at a casino, with a bucket of nickels as big as a swimming pool. Betty's not too proud to poke fun at her own image—and that's just another reason we love her.

30 Rock (2009)

In one episode of the NBC sitcom *30 Rock* (which was, in part, inspired by *The Mary Tyler Moore Show*), star Tracy Jordan calls Betty White to check that she's still alive—by yelling into the phone! Not only is she still kicking, she's feistier than ever:

"Tracy! I haven't seen you since that rapping grandma movie we did," she says, when she answers the phone. "You were so funny as the rapping grandma!" She quickly figures out that he's calling to see how she's doing because two other celebrities have recently died. "Is this a 'rule of threes' call?" she asks. He says no, but it's clear he's lying. "Nice try, Jordan, but I am going to be at your funeral. I will bury you!" she yells into the phone before hanging up on him.

My Name Is Earl (2009)

In a one-episode guest appearance in the fourth season of the comedy, White plays the "Crazy Witch Lady" who locks Earl (Jason Lee) and everyone else who has ever wronged her down in the basement (yes, it's a comedy!). The part earned the actress her eighteenth Emmy nomination (Outstanding Guest Actress in a Comedy). She lost out to Tina Fey, who won for a *Saturday Night Live* appearance. The following year, Fey would lose the same award to White.

Animated Roles

Given she's always been such an animated character, it makes perfect sense that White voiced a slew of animated characters in both TV series and feature films throughout the years.

✳ In the 1996 CBS animated TV special, *The Story of Santa Claus*, White provided the voice for Mrs. Claus alongside her old *Mary Tyler Moore Show* paramour Ed Asner as Santa Claus himself. Ho ho ho! Thankfully, Mrs. Claus is a lot less lecherous than Sue Ann Nivens.

✳ In 2016, White voiced Beatrice, a kindly older owner of a Grandma's Apron, a mall store under the sea on Nickelodeon's *SpongeBob SquarePants*. Her character comforts Pearl, who is being teased by a mean goth teen named Nocturna (voiced by Aubrey Plaza). "Don't let those bobble-headed nincompoops get to you, Pearly," White's character says, adding that she was teased when she was in school. "They called me Boring Beatrice. Not very creative, those girls."

✳ In 2012, Betty supplied the voice for Grammy Norma, Ted's (Zac Efron) grandma in *Dr. Seuss' The Lorax*, a new character created specifically for the movie. Even though everyone discounts her because of her age—and, let's be fair, she's a little flaky—Grammy Norma is more clued in than people think. She can connect Ted to the Once-ler, the notorious villain who chops down trees to make Thneeds, "the thing everyone needs." She's also pretty excitable. "Grammy goes a little over the top to make a point . . ." White says in a featurette to promote the film, "which is not at all like me in real life." Cut to Betty White playing the diva, yelling to unseen crew members: "I said chamomile tea!"

* Though she didn't have a leading role in the film, Betty's performance stood out, as usual. Her character in the film is one of the most popular, which you can measure by the viral memes of Grammy Norma. She was easily the coolest character in the film. As she sings in "Let It Grow," in the final musical number where the townsfolk joyously gather to plant a tree downtown, "I'm Grammy Norma, I'm old and I've got gray hair! But I remember when trees were everywhere!" Rock it, Grammy!

* She played herself in two episodes of *The Simpsons*. In "Missionary Impossible," she hosts a PBS pledge drive and accuses viewers of being crooks if they watched the network without contributing. Homer feels guilty and pledges ten thousand dollars—which he has no intention of paying. Betty tracks Homer down and sics a mob of angry PBS characters on Homer. "If you watch even one second of PBS and don't contribute, you are a thief. A common thief!" And Betty White is gonna get you.

* In "Homerazzi," Homer gets a job as a paparazzi photographer and finds that celebrities generally (and understandably) don't like having their photos snapped by paparazzi—except, Betty White! She greets him by

name and is happy to pose for a photo. She even has a self-addressed stamped envelope so he can send one of the pictures to her so she can sign it and send it back to him.

✳ In 2019, our animated heroine provided the voice for Bitey White, a teething toy with a tiger face, in Pixar's *Toy Story 4*, alongside her friend and fellow showbiz legends in the toy box including Carol Burnett, Mel Brooks, and Carl Reiner. At ninety-seven, White told *Entertainment Weekly* (*EW*) she was thrilled to be reuniting with her old pals. "It doesn't get any better."

Betty White's Movie Roles

Unlike most actors, our hard-working heroine never clamored to work on the stage or big screen. By the time she made her feature film debut as a senator in Otto Preminger's star-studded political drama *Advise & Consent*, in 1962, White was already a television veteran. Given the film starred bigger box office names at the time, such as Henry Fonda, Charles Laughton, Gene Tierney, and Burgess Meredith, it's not surprising that White's relatively small role didn't earn her much notice. Besides, she was working steadily on TV. As it turned out, she didn't return to the big screen for another thirty-six years! Even then, she wasn't offered the juicy roles. In 1998, she appeared in a couple of mediocre films in which she was underutilized: *Hard Rain*, a disaster-thriller starring Christian Slater, Morgan Freeman, and her old *MTM* costar Ed Asner, and *Dennis the Menace Strikes Again*.

With David E. Kelley's *Lake Placid* in 1999, White finally landed a feature film role she could dig her teeth into, so to speak. As Mrs. Delores Bickerman, a seemingly sweet old lady who feeds cows to a thirty-foot crocodile in a remote Maine lake—and is accused of murdering her husband—White revealed a gleefully foul-mouthed side.

"I was looking for the sweetest, most grandmotherly type, who in fact was vicious and had a gutter mouth. Betty certainly personified the former, and she had no problem embracing the latter," the film's director David E. Kelly told *EW* in 1999. The film received generally terrible reviews, but Betty's performance stood out, partially because of her character's crude language, which audiences found hilariously incongruous coming out of her mouth. When the local sheriff asks if she killed her husband, she answers: "If I had a dick, this is where I would tell you to suck it."

It wasn't until *The Proposal* in 2009, where White played saucy, brutally honest, sexually frank Grandma Annie aka Gammy, that she experienced her first genuine box office hit. The romantic comedy starring Sandra Bullock and Ryan Reynolds raked in more than $317 million worldwide, making it the twentieth highest-grossing film of the year. The plot revolves around Margaret Tate (Bullock), a Canadian career woman and demanding boss who connives her personal assistant, Andrew (Reynolds), into a shotgun wedding so she can stay in the U.S. after her work visa expires. Andrew reluctantly agrees to the sham marriage, but first Margaret has to attend a family wedding with Andrew in Alaska.

As Andrew's "Gammy," White was "only" a supporting player, but the scenes she appears in are among the film's most memorable—and outrageous ones—like when she first meets Margaret and asks her, in the most chipper way, "Now do you prefer being called Margaret or Satan's Mistress?"

Hardcore fans of the film can, no doubt, recite Betty's lines from the scene where Gammy tries to fit Margaret in her old wedding dress. "Let's see if we can find your boobs," she says as she feels Margaret up. "They're in there somewhere! This is like an Easter egg hunt!" Her face brightens as she smiles her dimply (and devilish) Betty White smile. That scene earned her an MTV Movie nomination for "Best WTF Moment."

On the character of Grandma Annie, White told the *NY Daily News* that she's "a rather normal lady most of the time, but she also thinks she's a shaman." Since the character really wants to get Andrew and Margaret to start a family, she does a special fertility dance around the fire. The actress even learned some of the Tlingit language for (sort of) accuracy. "You have to almost memorize it syllable by syllable," she said.

"You wouldn't expect her to do and say these nasty [things]— it belies her physical look and age," said David Hoberman, producer of *The Proposal*. "It's what makes her so funny." The role introduced her to a new audience and propelled her to an entirely new level of fame— at age eighty-seven! Critics called her a "scene stealer."

Even more important to Betty than the reviews, she had a blast starring alongside A-listers Bullock and Reynolds, and they fell in love with her. "We hated to see the movie end. We hated to part with each other," White told CBS News' *The Early Show*.

They had so much fun during production, the funny trio happily reteamed for a behind-the-scenes comedy video for FunnyorDie.com where White treats Reynolds like a gopher and bosses him around. "When Betty White says she wants a cup of coffee, you get her a (bleep) in' cup of coffee, you ab-crunching jackass!"

Her costars were similarly enthralled by working with her and credit her with making *The Proposal* a hit. "She is this sweet sort of lovable character with an edge, and we exploited that edge over and over and over again on that film," Reynolds said in the PBS documentary *Betty White: First Lady of Television*. "I don't think that film would have been nearly as successful or effective without her presence." Reynolds recounted a story about the unexpected joys of working with White:

> She's a rascal. She's just this sweet, you know, lovely older woman who is just beloved by the whole crew and cast that everybody would just do anything for her, and she gets up to leave, and everyone's sad 'cuz it's her last shot, and she's just walking out the door to say goodbye, and she turns around, right in the doorjamb and she says, "I just want everyone here to know this is the most fun I've ever had . . . standing up," and then she turns and I mean, just the woman just kills everyone. Everybody spends the rest of the day at a perfect 90-degree angle laughing.

BETTY WHITE TRIVIA: Betty's *Mary Tyler Moore Show* castmate Cloris Leachman replaced her in *Lake Placid 2*, the 2007 made-for-television sequel to the 1999 original feature. Leachman plays Sadie, the crazy sister of Betty's memorably tart-tongued character, Delores Bickerman.

Betty's Work Rules:

✳ **Give it your all.** Even if it's not your dream job, don't phone it in. Remember: Every opportunity is a chance to shine. Okay, maybe you won't always glisten, but you'll work hard and do your best because you're a professional.

✳ **Don't badmouth your coworkers.** Betty always knew better than to speak ill of any of her colleagues or to spread gossip. It would just create drama that would detract from the work. That doesn't mean she never mumbled anything under her breath or saved it to talk it over with Allen.

✳ **Don't take all the credit.** Even after all of the awards and the nonstop praise, Betty always credited the writers and her coworkers with all of her success. There's no need to be that modest, but be sure to let others know you appreciate their work.

✳ **Follow your dream, but be open to alternatives.** Betty always knew she wanted to be in show business, but she was open to a variety of opportunities (becoming a forest ranger and an author!).

✳ **Don't forget the basics.** No matter how successful or famous you may be, be like Betty and show up prepared and on time. Betty never had patience for actors who showed up late and unprepared. Nobody wants to deal with a diva.

The Betty White "Diet"

When you live as long—and as robustly—as Betty White, it's only natural that people want to know your super power. Time and time again, interviewers have enquired whether the secret to her longevity lies in her diet. She doesn't have a "special diet" unless you count junk food as a "special diet." Her longtime favorites are potato chips and hot dogs. The famous Pink's hot dog stand in California even named a hot dog after her. Since she likes her hot dogs plain, they called it the Betty White "Naked" Dog.

* While Betty doesn't have much of a sweet tooth (aside from Snickers! And Red Vines! And Pepsi!), she is known to enjoy a cocktail before or after dinner. "Vodka's kind of a hobby," she told David Letterman in 2011 soon after she turned eighty-nine. Letterman whipped out two glasses and filled them with Grey Goose vodka (animal lover that she is, that's her favorite). And yes, they did shots.

* Betty's attitude toward physical fitness isn't much better than her diet. Her exercise regimen: "I have a two-story house and a very bad memory, so I'm up and down those stairs." Better than nothing, but hardly enough movement to sustain an ordinary mortal. Betty is lucky to have the constitution of an ox. Makes you wonder what kind of cows they were milking back in St. Olaf. Or in Los Angeles!

How Well Do You Know Rose?

The character of Rose is more complex than you might assume, full of surprise random talents and eccentric interests. She's a sci-fi fan, who can reference *Star Trek*, as well as a tap dancer, a die-hard *Miami Vice* fan, and a competent plumber! Her hobbies include cheese making, stamp collecting, and Viking history! Her résumé reads like a Swiss army knife: one of everything. There's probably a jet pilot's license in there and a stint as a rodeo clown. Use your imagination. Just when you think you know what Rose is capable of, she proves you wrong. To see how well you know Rose, test your knowledge of St. Olaf's Woman of the Year:

1. Rose never knew who her biological parents were. When she finally meets her biological father during her candy striping rounds, she learns that he is a/an:
    a. Actor
    b. Doctor
    c. Monk
    d. Rabbi

2. Rose claims that while she was growing up in St. Olaf, she was taught by:
    a. Hitler
    b. Abraham Lincoln
    c. Jimmy Carter
    d. Bob Hope

3. Rose discovers that her boyfriend Miles is being pursued by:
   a. The Mafia
   b. His ex-wife
   c. The IRS
   d. The police

4. Rose meets Blanche for the first time at:
   a. A doctor's waiting room
   b. Driver's Ed
   c. A mutual friend's housewarming party
   d. A supermarket

5. Rose has held all of the following jobs except _____.
   a. Grief counselor
   b. Waitress
   c. Associate TV producer
   d. Teacher

6. Rose talks about her children, but we only see two of them throughout the series run. How many does she have?
   a. Two
   b. Three
   c. Four
   d. Five

7. In her high school class, Rose was voted:

   a. Most likely to get stuck in a tuba

   b. Most likely to work with farm animals

   c. Queen of St. Olaf

   d. Smartest

8. Rose is worried that she ___ men when they have sex.

   a. Disappoints

   b. Kills

   c. Bores

   d. Intimidates

9. All of the following are real St. Olaf traditions except _____.

   a. Hay Day

   b. The Crowning of the Princess Pig

   c. The Day of the Wheat

   d. The Festival of the Dancing Piglets

10. When she was a teenager, classmates used to call her:

   a. Rose with the hairy legs

   b. Rose with the milking cow

   c. Rose of St. Olaf

   d. Rose with the small brain

Add up your responses.

If you got between 0–4 points: You call yourself a *Golden Girls* fan? You need to study up on the ladies from Miami and in particular Rose. She deserves some attention!

If you got between 5–7 points: You're a respectable *Golden Girls* fan. Maybe you haven't seen every episode—or maybe it's been years since you did, but you still remember what makes Rose special. Well done!

If you got between 8–10 points: You're a true *Golden Girls* fan and you know more about the Girl from St. Olaf than almost anyone. Go ahead and be like Rose and blow your own Geneuckenfluegen!

CHAPTER EIGHT

IT AIN'T OVER 'TIL IT'S OVER— REINVENT YOURSELF

"2010 TURNED OUT TO BE, AS THEY SAY, a very good year," White wrote in her memoir *If You Ask Me (And of Course You Won't)*. "Very good" would be just a bit of an understatement. More like "outstanding" or "unbelievable." In a decades-long career punctuated by many highs, at eighty-eight, she hit a career pinnacle— and won over an entirely new generation of fans. Still riding the wave of "newfound" success generated by *The Proposal*, White kicked the year off by accepting a SAG Lifetime Achievement Award in January in her typical tongue-in-cheek fashion. The crowd ate it up and begged for more!

"Thank you from the bottom of my heart and the bottom of my bottom," she said.

When her *Proposal* costar and friend Sandra Bullock presented her with the award, White teased, "Isn't it heartening to see how far a girl as plain as she is can go?"

In classic Betty White double entendre, she told attendees: "I look out into this audience, and I see so many famous faces. But what really boggles my mind is that I actually know many of you and have worked with quite a few. Maybe *had* a couple—and you know who you are!" Ahem.

Speaking about her long career, she mused about the importance of enthusiasm. "I often wonder about people who don't have some kind of passion, something that they care so deeply about that it never fails to fascinate them," she told the audience. "How lucky can I be to have two such passions: show business and animals. Actually, I may have more than two passions, but that's none of your business!" Saucy!

Betty's hot streak continued the next day on TBS's *Lopez Tonight*. When host George Lopez commented that she's working more than ever, she answered: "I'm such a whore. I can't say no." Lopez and the audience convulsed into hysterical laughter that reignited when he congratulated her on her SAG Award. "I wish they wouldn't call it sag!" she said, grasping her chest.

Just when it seemed like Betty White–mania couldn't get any hotter, a Snickers commercial that aired during Super Bowl XLIV catapulted her to mega-fame. Suddenly, Betty White was everywhere—even she was getting worried about being overexposed. But the world couldn't get enough of her. Nobody can remember who won the Super Bowl, but everyone remembers the Snickers ad that went viral—around the world—thanks to White's performance.

In the "You're Not You When You're Hungry" ad, the Golden Girl is playing a rough game of tackle football with a group of young jocks who are miffed by her apparent lack of athletic skills. She misses a pass, gets tackled, and lands splat in a mud puddle. When she gets back to the huddle, a teammate asks: "Mike, what is your deal, man?" "Oh, come on, man, you've been riding me all day," Betty growls back. "You're playing like Betty White out there," says another player. "That's not what your girlfriend says," she snaps back. But, wait, it's not Betty, it's Mike's hungry alter ego. Once she takes a bite of a Snickers candy bar, Betty magically morphs back into Mike.

James Miller, global head of strategy for Mars at BBDO, the advertising giant behind the Snickers ad, credited Betty with the commercial's outsized success. "It prompted such a groundswell of enthusiasm that, ultimately, we received more than ninety-one days of media coverage from one thirty-second ad. We were famous," said Miller, who noted that when White appeared on *The Tonight Show Starring Jay Leno*, *The Oprah Winfrey Show*, *Larry King Live*, and *The Ellen DeGeneres Show*, they all played clips from the Snickers ad. Can't buy that sort of free advertising!

Of course, more than all of that, the ad—along with Betty—was incorporated into just about every element of pop culture, including memes and other viral social media content. The Super Bowl XLIV commercial won the top spot on *USA Today*'s "Super Bowl Ad Meter" and, more importantly, helped to fuel the Betty White–aissance that had already begun with *The Proposal*.

White later said she hadn't expected the ad to go viral—certainly, not when they were filming it. "The idea was, I was playing football with a group of nice young men. (Tough duty!) It wound up with me being tackled into a pool of icy, muddy water. A great stuntwoman took the actual tackle, and I just lay down in the puddle in the same position where she had landed. She took the dive, but I got the laugh. Sure doesn't seem fair, does it?" As always, Betty was incredibly humble and took no credit for the well-earned laughs she got with her hilarious performance in the ad.

The rest of the month only got wilder: Betty White hopped in the shower with Hugh Jackman on *The Tonight Show with Jay Leno*, got a lap dance from Chippendales' dancers on *Ellen,* and told Larry King she didn't know the meaning of the word "retirement." Jay Leno rightfully declared White "America's biggest star."

What Comeback?

Big comeback? She was working all along!

"I didn't know I'd been away, and then all of a sudden that Snickers commercial kind of turned a lot of other things on," she told Oprah.com. "Now I'm busier than I've ever been." The truth is that Betty's career has never slowed down. Betty's IMDb listing shows screen credits for almost every single year from 1953 to 2019!

Even before the Super Bowl ad aired, David Matthews, a twenty-nine-year-old Betty White fan in San Antonio, Texas, created a Facebook page to get her to host *SNL*. After the flurry of publicity surrounding the Snickers ad, the Facebook campaign gained traction. By March, the page had more than half a million fans.

Soon after, *SNL* announced that the former *Golden Girl* would host! *SNL* creator Lorne Michaels hadn't been swayed by the Facebook campaign. In fact, he had invited White to host the show several times in the past, but she always had declined, saying she was too much of a California girl for the New York show. But this time around, her manager told her "in no uncertain terms" that she should do it! And she agreed.

On May 8, 2010, the California girl hosted the quintessential New York show for the first time at age eighty-eight, making her the show's oldest host ever. *SNL* alumnae Rachel Dratch, Tina Fey, Ana Gasteyer, Amy Poehler, Maya Rudolph, and Molly Shannon returned for the special "Mother's Day" episode. They were all eager to get the chance to work with their favorite comic goddess!

Not surprisingly, after decades of ad-libbing on live television and on game shows, White's comic timing was spot-on, and she excelled on *SNL*. "When I first heard about the campaign to get me to host *Saturday Night Live*, I didn't know what Facebook was," White riffed in her opening monologue. "Now that I know what it is, it sounds like a huge waste of time. I wouldn't say the people on it are losers, but that's because I'm polite."

She continued: "Needless to say, we didn't have Facebook when I was growing up. We had phone books, but you wouldn't waste an afternoon on them."

In an NPR parody, White played alongside Molly Shannon and Ana Gasteyer as Florence Dusty, a "rock star in the confectionery world"— who brought her famous giant muffin. "Many bakers from my era have dry or even yeasty muffins," said White . . . and many double entendres followed. The show's musical guest Jay-Z later performed his latest single, "Young Forever," which he dedicated to "the most incredible Betty White."

Everyone agreed that she rocked it—in total Betty White fashion. When asked about what it was like working with the octogenerian, cast member Will Forte shared this story:

She got in super-early on Friday, worked all day, then went
to bed at about 12:30. She's eighty-eight-and-a-half! So the
next day I said, "How are you doing? Did you get some sleep?"
And she said, "Oh, I don't need sleep. I just went to my hotel
and had a cold hot dog and a vodka on the rocks." Which was
exactly what I wanted Betty White to say.

Not only did her *SNL* performance earn rave reviews, but the show drew its highest ratings in eighteen months. The episode was also one of *SNL*'s most buzzed about on social media. Even Justin Bieber tweeted, "BETTY WHITE RULES." White's buddy Ryan Reynolds later gushed, "I can't believe Betty did *SNL* at that age and not only did *SNL* at that age, but took the ball and knocked it so far out of the park." Tina Fey said it "was inspiring just to see that her timing is rock solid, still." The appearance also earned the octogenarian the seventh Emmy Award of her career (don't worry, we've lost track, too!).

"All it took to reinvigorate a 35-year-old comedy show was the presence of an 88-year-old woman," noted the *New York Times* about her *SNL* appearance. "Despite Ms. White's opening monologue, which made distinctions between her generation and that of the *SNL* fans who pushed for her to host, she seemed at home on the show."

The Betty White lovefest continued, with Ellen DeGeneres telling Betty on *Ellen*, "I don't know if there's anyone who's more loved than you." When DeGeneres asked what it's like to have 500,000 petition to have her host *Saturday Night Live*, White replied: "Five hundred thousand? That's more people than I've dated!"

It seemed everyone wanted a piece of Betty White (except for Robert Redford, as she'd frequently joke). She told Jay Leno the tawdry details of her handsy encounter with Jay-Z on *Saturday Night Live*. "He just got desperate, I guess!" She had so much fun on *SNL*—and was such a hit—that she was invited back for its fortieth anniversary in 2015, where she was featured in a soap opera spoof called "The Californians," along with Taylor Swift, Kerry Washington, Kristen Wiig, and Bill Hader. Even better, Betty got to make out with Bradley Cooper!

At eighty-eight, she was getting more TV and movie roles than ever, including in the Walt Disney Pictures comedy *You Again* alongside Kristen Bell, Jamie Lee Curtis, and Sigourney Weaver. White got a huge kick out of meeting Weaver since she had worked with her father, Pat Weaver, when he was president of NBC and she landed her first network job, *The Betty White Show*, more than half a century earlier! "Sigourney wasn't even a gleam in her father's eye at that time." Life's funny that way, isn't it?

Hot in Cleveland . . . and Everywhere Else

White got yet another offer too juicy to refuse: cable network TV Land, which was known for airing classic TV shows, was developing its first original sitcom, *Hot in Cleveland*. The show's premise centered around three single "women of a certain age" who abandoned their glamorous careers in Los Angeles to move to Cleveland, where they are considered hot. The women rent a house in town that, in classic sitcom style, comes with a cranky tough-talking hard-drinking caretaker with a mysterious past, Elka Ostrovsky.

The producers had already assembled the perfect cast featuring sitcom veterans Wendie Malick (*Just Shoot Me*), Valerie Bertinelli (*One Day at a Time*), and Jane Leeves (*Frasier*) to play the Los Angelenos. They knew the perfect person to play Elka: Betty White. She agreed to do the pilot, with the understanding that she would not be involved if it was picked up as a series. But when the show was an instant success and TV Land begged her to do more episodes, how could Betty say no?! She ended up appearing in every episode of the show.

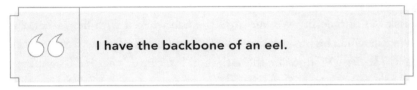

I have the backbone of an eel.

For White, it was like Old Home Week since *Hot in Cleveland* was shot in front of a live studio audience at the CBS Studio Center in Studio City, the same studio where *The Mary Tyler Moore Show* had been filmed more than thirty years earlier. Not surprisingly, when the series premiered, critics compared it to *The Golden Girls*. Original it was not. That wasn't the point. If anything, *Hot in Cleveland* harkened back to the saucy punch lines and predictable zingers of the sitcoms that the show's stars had previously appeared in. As the first original scripted comedy on TV Land, a network founded on reruns, the *New York Times*' Alessandra Stanley wrote, "*Hot in Cleveland* is a pastiche of classics—a little bit *Cheers* and *Frasier*, a little bit *The Golden Girls*."

In fact, *Hot in Cleveland*'s creator Suzanne Martin said the concept for the new show came to her while watching clips from *The Golden Girls* after star Estelle Getty died in 2008. Just as Harris was excited to write about issues facing "older women" on *The Golden Girls*, Martin was "inspired to think about what pushing fifty looks like now and what it didn't look like then."

Curious to see some of their favorite "classic" sitcom stars working together in an updated *Golden Girls* setup, the audience tuned in. When *Hot in Cleveland* premiered on June 16, 2010, it was TV Land's highest-rated telecast in its fourteen-year-history (4.75 million viewers tuned in for the premiere). The show would continue for six successful seasons.

White's Elka, with her nasty one-liners and outrageous life story, quickly became a fan favorite. White was once again playing a naughty old lady pushing everybody's buttons. But nobody plays that role with as much flair as she does. Her unexpected delivery and sly humor added complexity to the part, which, in less experienced hands, could have easily been one-note.

Elka is certainly more like conniving Sue Ann than sweet, naive Rose. In one episode, Elka dresses in mourner's black and attends the funeral of a stranger because it's a good way to meet men. When "the girls" point out she's already got a boyfriend, she responds: "Just because you're chained to the fence doesn't mean you can't bark at the car." That's totally something Sue Ann would do.

But in lots of ways, Elka is more like Sophia Petrillo, the cranky old lady who has no verbal filter, played by Estelle Getty on *The Golden Girls*. Like Sophia, Elka says whatever comes into her mind—without considering how it might be received. Like Sophia, Elka tells it like it is!

When she's not bedazzling her tracksuits or preparing for a date, Elka is busy putting the girls down. One of the main targets of Elka's nasty zingers is Joy Scroggs (Jane Leeves), a never-married beautician known as the "Eyebrow Queen of Beverly Hills." One running gag is that Elka, nearly ninety, gets way more "action" than Joy.

In season two, the "girls" take a trip to L.A. and Elka, like White, is obsessed with finding Robert Redford. Like White, Elka turns on the charm and shows off her dimples when she wants to get her way. The show becomes super-meta when Elka talks her way onto Jimmy Kimmel's show, where he dubs her "the Cleveland granny." On another visit to L.A., she tries to convince Mario Lopez (who appeared on a 1987 episode of *The Golden Girls*!) to shoot *Extra* in Cleveland. She's so aggressive that she loses her L.A. driving privileges for flipping off Tom Hanks. It's not her fault if "Forrest Gump drives like a soccer mom!"

Like Betty, Elka can't get enough naughty double entendres—and it's often unclear if she understands what she's blurting out. In one episode, Elka gets a match on a dating website—she signed up when her booze bender was over . . . "In fact, that's my screen name . . . Bender Over," she tells the girls, seemingly without understanding why they're cracking up. Still, there's always that gleam in Betty White's eyes, which makes you wonder.

"Working with Betty White really is like having a master class of comedic timing," said Bertinelli, who played Melanie on *Hot in Cleveland*. "She gets it. It's a gift that she has. She's honed it over quite a few years."

LIFE LESSON:

Old Friends Are the Best Friends

One of the best parts about working on *Hot in Cleveland* was that it allowed White to reunite with old costars and dear friends such as Carl Reiner, as well as Joan Rivers, who showed up in one episode as Elka's twin sister, Anka!

Betty and Joan had become friends on the talk-show/game-show circuit, where they each represented the fairer sex with panache and humor. When Joan Rivers hosted her own talk show in 1990, who did she invite on as a regular guest? Betty, of course. And now Betty was eager to have her old friend show up for a cameo on her show.

"What have you done to your face?" Elka asks her twin, who's clearly gotten a lot of "work" done to her face. "Where's the famous Ostrovsky neck freckle?"

"Oh, please, after five face lifts, it's on my forehead!" Anka replies, noting Elka's wrinkles. "Natural aging. Disgusting!"

The "twins" haven't talked in forty years, but they forgot what caused their rift.

"Was it when I pretended to be you and slept with your boyfriend?" Anka asks.

"Was it when I pretended to be you and escaped from Poland?" asks Elka.

In the second season premiere, Mary Tyler Moore guest starred as Elka's cellmate in jail following Elka's arrest in the first season finale. It marked the first time since the series finale of *The Mary Tyler Moore Show* in 1977 that the two friends appeared on-screen together. Looking very *Orange Is the New Black* in her orange prison-issued jumpsuit, Betty plays harmonica and sings the jailhouse blues: "Nobody Knows the Trouble I've Seen." As her cellmate, Moore's character has a signature *M* up on the prison wall behind her (just like Mary Richards had on her apartment wall on *The Mary Tyler Moore Show*). Apparently, in this case, the *M* stands for *Murder*.

Thirty-five years after *The Mary Tyler Moore Show* wrapped, Georgia Engel, who played the dim-witted, sweet Georgette, joined the third season of *Hot in Cleveland* as Mamie Sue Johnson, Elka's best friend, in a recurring role. When Mamie and Elka start an illegal pharmacy, they end up asking a local mobster and his mother for help. The mobster was played by none other than William Shatner of *Star Trek* fame and his mother was played by *The Partridge Family* matriarch Shirley Jones. Perfect casting for a show airing on a cable network devoted to classic television!

Moore returned to Cleveland one more time, along with her *Mary Tyler Moore Show* costars Cloris Leachman and Valerie Harper. The former castmates played former members of Elka and Mamie's bowling team, "The Gorgeous Ladies of Bowling" or "GLOB," which disbanded following a fallout after their 1963 championship–winning season fifty years earlier.

After hearing that Valerie Harper, who had played Rhoda, was seriously ill, *Hot in Cleveland* creator Martin created a reunion episode to bring the costars of *The Mary Tyler Moore Show* together one final time. The show turned out to be Moore's final acting role and one of Valerie Harper's last as well. "It was magical. It was as if no time had passed," said the show's executive producer Todd Milliner. "The episode was called 'Love Is All Around,' and it really, really was that night."

White's *Hot in Cleveland* role earned her two consecutive SAG wins for Outstanding Performance by a Female Actor in a Comedy Series (2011 and 2012) and yet another Emmy nomination. The show wrapped in 2015 with a two-part series finale that neatly tied up the characters' story lines, with happy endings for all, including a wedding for Elka. She ends up marrying Joy's fiancé Bob's father (played by none other than Emmy winner Bob Newhart) in a double wedding ceremony. It marked a reunion for Betty White and Bob Newhart, who had costarred in the second season of the short-lived series *Bob*, which aired on CBS in the early 1990s.

After the wedding, when Joy and Bob formalize the adoption of their daughter, they decide to name her Elizabeth. They call her Betty for short, a sweet nod to Betty White. "Everything you can imagine about working with Betty White every day for six seasons—what you would dream that to be like—doesn't even touch what it's really like," said Martin. "We love her so much, and she inspired everyone, every day. When I thought of naming the baby that, I started to tear up. I thought, 'OK, that works and that makes sense.'"

For White, the show marked the third time she was part of an award-winning, hit sitcom ensemble featuring amazingly talented women. "What absolutely boggles my mind is that I find myself in yet another hit series, having a ball with a wonderful cast and crew. One of those in a lifetime is a blessing, two of them is a privilege, but three out of three? I owe Someone big time," she said.

Classic Elka-isms

Did Elka really say that? Yes, the character of Elka can say some pretty outrageous and sometimes downright offensive things. Some of them are pretty hard to believe. Did Elka really say that? Yes, chances are good that she did. Below are ten of the best—by which we mean worst—Elka doozies!

1. "The truth is I'm a great driver, but sometimes I like to drive real slow just to mess with people."

2. "Sweats, pizza, and wine—it's like the cover of *Giving Up* magazine."

3. "Nice girls keep their cookies in a jar."

4. "I feel like an energetic forty-year-old—in fact,
   I could go for one right now."

5. "Don't put yourself down, dear—that's my job."

6. "Escaping from the Nazis was the least of my worries."

7. "It was just one polka. It didn't mean anything."

8. "I've never been in a triangle before. You girls are slutty.
   What would you do?"

9. "My preschool was a box. My teacher was a potato.
   And winter came . . . and I had to eat my teacher!"

10. "In your twenties you dress for men, in your forties
    you dress for success, in your eighties you dress
    for a bathroom."

CHAPTER NINE

AGING IS JUST A MINDSET

EVEN WAY BACK IN 1974, WHEN SHE JOINED the cast of *The Mary Tyler Moore Show* as the man-crazy "older woman" Sue Ann Nivens in the show's fourth season, Betty was already fifty-two years old and was pleasantly surprised to have a "late-career" hit. Little did she know that 1974 wasn't even mid-career. She would go on to have many "late-career" hits. Betty was sixty-three when *The Golden Girls* kicked off its run in 1985. By the time *Hot in Cleveland* premiered in 2010, she was eighty-eight! That same year, she became the oldest person to ever host *SNL*.

She's the rare celebrity who gained fame as she aged. She was more popular in her eighties than she was in her twenties! So she gives the rest of us hope. Betty has no secret to longevity, but she has long said aging is about "your mental attitude. So many of us start dreading age in high school, and that's a waste of a lovely life. 'Oh . . . I'm thirty, oh, I'm forty, oh, fifty.' Make the most of it." Of course, it helps that White has been blessed with good health, but regardless, she always focuses on the positive. "A lot of people think this is a Goody Two-shoes talking," she said. "But we do have a tendency to complain rather than celebrating who we are. I learned at my mother's knee it's better to appreciate what's happening . . . I think we kind of talk ourselves into the negative sometimes." That healthy attitude has kept Betty going and going and . . .

Even an optimist like Betty realizes that having a positive attitude won't help pay your rent or cure you if you're sick. She knows she's incredibly lucky to have led the amazing life she's led. It's easier to "focus on the positive" when you have a nice big house or two and enough money to guarantee you'll get the best care.

Chatting with Alan Alda on his podcast in 2020, she said it's good to focus on the positive, but "don't be a pain in the ass doing it— because people get fed up with that very quickly!" It's true. Focusing on the positive doesn't mean forgetting the reality of your current situation. As usual, Betty even came up with a joke on the topic. "If you hear someone has six months to live, don't say, 'Well, at least now you know your schedule'!" She loved to defy stereotypes about age. She's proof that we don't have to age like our parents did. We can push limits into our eighties and beyond. And "don't be a pain in the ass" is generally good life advice to follow.

So while we're fretting about our expanding waistlines and graying hair, there will be Betty, always older than us and always sassier. Her brand of humor never goes out of style. The "dirty old broad" makes aging look fun! Unlike most mortals who count the days until they can retire, White counts the hours until she can get back to work, back on set, cracking wise. She's a self-proclaimed workaholic, but she loves what she does so much, it doesn't feel like work. "I rarely hear the alarm clock," she wrote. "Even when I have to get up early, I usually awake before it goes off. I need about four hours' deep sleep, and I'm good to go. I chalk it up to my passions and enthusiasm. I can't imagine living any other way."

So whenever you're getting tired and you're thinking of leaning back from the world, just remember Betty, and lean in. Or bend over, if that's more comfortable.

LIFE LESSON:

Stay Active and Keep Doing What You Love

Starring in *Hot in Cleveland* wasn't enough to keep White busy. She wanted to pack in as much work as possible, working with people she liked on projects that meant something to her. When the show was on hiatus, Betty couldn't resist taking on side projects she was excited about, including a fun role on the NBC comedy *Community* (see below) and a leading role opposite Jennifer Love Hewitt (*Party of Five*) in the Hallmark Hall of Fame movie *The Lost Valentine*.

She was nearly eighty-nine—or as she put it "eighty-eight-and-three-quarters years old" when she flew to Atlanta to shoot the movie, and it was worth the effort. In the film, Hewitt plays a reporter who interviews White about her husband, who she's been pining for since he was declared Missing in Action during World War II.

Doing a love story was "a nice change of pace," and the project appealed to her because it was about a lost love. "It's a deep, deep love story, like the one I had with my beloved Allen Ludden."

She had a great time filming the movie in Atlanta. Knowing she's a big animal lover, all of the neighbors brought their dogs to visit her on set! "We'd look across the street from the set, and they'd all be lined up—owners and dogs, sitting on the wall. Between scenes, I'd go across the street to say hello and get to know all the dogs," she recalled. "I got my dog fix every day. Now, that's a happy set."

The movie premiered on CBS on January 30, 2011, the same night that White was picking up her SAG Award as Best Actress in a TV Comedy Series for her role on *Hot in Cleveland*. *The Lost Valentine* was a surprise ratings hit! Nearly 15 million people tuned in, making it the most-watched Hallmark movie in four years. "Want TV ratings? Hire Betty White, CBS Finds" read one headline.

Though the script got so-so reviews, Betty received raves for her subtle, heartbreaking performance. "The only reason to tune in for *The Lost Valentine* is, of course, Betty White," wrote Matthew Gilbert in the *Boston Globe*. "It's just nice to see her doing a role that enables her to bring her age and experience into play. She's a funny lady for sure, but she can also nicely manage gravitas and vulnerability."

The role earned White a SAG nomination for Outstanding Performance by a Female Actor in a Television Movie or Miniseries. She lost out to Kate Winslet (*Mildred Pierce*), but White had nothing to cry about: She won another SAG award that night for Outstanding Performance by a Female Actor in a Comedy Series for her work on *Hot in Cleveland*.

Even when Betty "loses," she wins.

She's Still Hot

Right around the time that TV Land picked up a second season of *Hot in Cleveland*, White accepted a recurring guest spot on the NBC series *Community* as the eccentric anthropology professor June Bauer. The nutty professor drinks her own urine and relishes hunting big game, including smug ex-lawyer Jeff Winger (Joel McHale), whom she attacks with a homemade crossbow. At the end of one episode, White's June joins Troy (Donald Glover, aka Childish Gambino) and nerd Abed (Danny Pudi) for an "Anthropology Rap" set to Toto's classic '80s anthem "Africa."

After showing off her rapping skills on *Community*, White kept the beat going. In October 2011, she did her first rap video. A collaboration with the Brit dance-pop artist Luciana, White hammed it up in the video for Luciana's hit "I'm Still Hot." She held her own, laying down raps opposite the much younger Luciana. Romping around with half-nude hunks, feeding them cheesecake, tangling with a boa constrictor, Betty showed us that she's still smokin' hot. It was all for charity, of course. The video was meant to raise awareness for the Lifeline Program, with a large portion of proceeds from iTunes music downloads benefiting the Los Angeles Zoo, one of White's "pet" projects.

On the verge of ninety, White literally became the "poster girl" for a new AARP advertising campaign featuring her looking and acting as vibrant as ever along with the tag line "Just get over it." White showed off her sassy attitude talking to reporters about the AARP campaign. "The message is, you can't get rid of me," she said. Not that we'd want to!

But wait . . . there's more. The first lady of television wasn't ready to retire. In fact, she was eager to take on new challenges. Acting in your senior years is more than most of us could handle, but Betty, at ninety, wasn't content to merely work in front of the camera; she was working (her butt off!) behind the lens, too. In 2013, she launched *Off Their Rockers*, a hidden camera show à la *Punk'd* or *Candid Camera,* where the elderly play pranks on younger generations (that'll show you, you young whippersnappers!). White served as the executive producer and on-screen host of the reality series, which was adapted from a popular Belgian series.

In addition to being featured in the occasional sketch, White shared her comic gems and sassy commentary with the audience at home. At the start of one of the episodes, Betty White tells the audience: "When I heard about all these television shows on the air today about hypersexual beings that don't age and live forever, I was surprised to find out that all these shows are about vampires. I thought they were finally making *The Betty White Story!*" Oh, Betty!

Sex and the Older Woman

She's still hot all right! According to Betty, you're never too old for sexual desire. "I don't have a fella, but if Allen—or Robert Redford—were around, we'd have a very active sex life," she told *AARP The Magazine* in 2010 at age eighty-eight. "Sexual desire is like aging—a lot of it's up here [points to her head]."

She also proves that sex appeal doesn't have an expiration date. While Robert Pattinson (*Twilight*) was promoting a movie on *The View* in 2010, the hosts asked the actor, then twenty-three, if he'd date an older woman. His response? "I think Betty White is probably one of the sexiest women in America. She's vibrant; it's sexy. I think the more age, the better." We're waiting for the sex scene, Robert!

Of course, one of the reasons White has gotten away with saying the bawdy things she does is because we're not always sure if she understands what she's saying—and that's part of the humor. During her appearance on his podcast in 2020, Betty's friend Alan Alda (*M*A*S*H*) praised her for her skill "at creating this character that the world loves you for and you're super sweet and you're saucy and spicy saucy." Her saucy response proves his point: "I don't think I'm spicy. I think that's a load of crap. I'm a dirty old broad is what I am!"

The characters White portrayed on *The Mary Tyler Moore Show*, *The Golden Girls*, and *Hot in Cleveland* still enjoyed active sex lives—and weren't shy about talking about it! Elka's got a lot of Sue Ann Nivens's sexual bravado. When Elka says, "I have had the feeling that someone is mentally undressing me, but for me, that's not unusual," it's almost as if she's channeling her inner Sue Ann. When she's on trial for theft (due to her mobster husband's hiding loot in the basement), Elka takes a juror into the closet to sway his opinion. When she exits a few minutes later, Elka adjusts her blouse and pronounces, "Justice has been serviced." Ahem.

Even naive Rose isn't as innocent as you might think. In one episode, she remarks that she can't remember all the boyfriends she had in St. Olaf since there were so many! In "Rose the Prude," in season one, her boyfriend Arnie (played by Harold Gould, who later reappears as Miles!) wants her to go on a cruise to the Bahamas with him. But Rose is nervous to be with a man "in that special way" for the first time since her husband, Charlie, died. It turns out she's afraid she'll kill him since Charlie died while they were making love!

Apparently, she and Charlie had quite a wild sex life. In season six, there's a drought in St. Olaf and the only way to end it is to be celibate. (Don't ask. Remember, it's St. Olaf!) The girls tell her she can take a break from sex, but Rose doesn't think she can abstain for long. "I don't think you realize how powerful sex is. Once Charlie and I actually did it 'til the cow came home," Rose tells the girls. And, of course, she means it literally!

Betty White's Thoughts on Aging

Over the years, she's demystified the idea of growing older and, with typical humor, helped us fear the aging process a little bit less. In 2011, the forever-young celebrity shared "Betty White's Tips for Living a Long and Happy Life" on *The Late Show with David Letterman*. Her tips included "helpful" tidbits such as "Get at least eight hours of beauty sleep—nine if you're ugly"; "Exercise. Or Don't. What the hell do I care?" And "Schedule nightly appointment with Dr. Johnnie Walker."

Those were her humorous "tips" for living a long and happy life. Below are ten of the smartest/funniest things she's said on the topic:

1. "My mother always told me never lie about your age. Brag about it! Never lie about it."

2. "You don't fall off the planet once you pass a given age. You don't lose any of your sense of humor. You don't lose any of your zest for life, or your lust for life, if you will!"

3. "I'm a teenager trapped in an old body."

4. "If you were a dull young person, you're going to be a dull old person."

5. "The image in your mirror may be a little disappointing, but if you are still functioning and not in pain, gratitude should be the name of the game."

6. "Somewhere along the line there is a breaking point, where you go from not discussing how old you are to bragging about it."

7. "There is even a funny side to aging, if one has a warped sense of humor. If one has no sense of humor, one is in trouble."

8. "One thing they don't tell you about growing old— you don't feel old, you just feel like yourself."

9. "Growing old is not for sissies."

10. My mother always used to say, "The older you get, the better you get. Unless you're a banana."

FUN FACT: The year 1922 was apparently a fertile year for creative types. In addition to Betty White, these are some of the other talents born that year: Judy Garland, Veronica Lake, Jack Kerouac, Ava Gardner, Doris Day, Bea Arthur, Dorothy Dandridge, Jack Klugman, Carl Reiner, Redd Foxx, Stan Lee, Ruby Dee, Telly Savalas, and Kurt Vonnegut Jr. Betty outlived them all!

Was Betty White Born Before . . .

Betty White's life and career have encompassed most of the twentieth century and a significant chunk of the twenty-first century. She's actually been around longer than some of our favorite everyday objects—think electric razors and computers. She's literally been around longer than sliced bread! So you could say that sliced bread is the best thing to come along since Betty White!

Take this quiz below to see how well you know what was invented after Betty White came into the world. Answer YES if the item is something that existed when Betty White was born in 1922 (don't worry, we're not counting months here). Answer NO if the item wasn't invented yet.

1. Frozen food
   YES   NO

2. Electric blender
   YES   NO

3. Polyester
   YES   NO

4. FM radio
   YES   NO

5. Instant coffee
   YES   NO

6. Air conditioning

   YES   NO

7. Ballpoint pens

   YES   NO

8. The Internet

   YES   NO

9. Jet engines

   YES   NO

10. Television

    YES   NO

Grow Older with Grace and Humor

Though the main goal was to be funny, *The Golden Girls* broke ground as the first prime-time show to focus on the lives of a group of female friends over fifty. It wasn't shy about tackling stereotypical attitudes about aging or wrapping humorous plot lines around decidedly unfunny topics, such as dementia, illness, disability, and euthanasia—not exactly popular issues for a prime-time sitcom.

The show's creator, Susan Harris, set out to take on difficult issues, as long as they were funny! But how do you make aging humorous? Harris was already a successful TV writer (*Maude, Benson, Soap*) who had broken barriers in prime time by tackling hot-button subjects. She wrote the famous "abortion" episode of *Maude* and created the character of Jodie Dallas, one of the first-ever openly gay character's in prime time (memorably played by newcomer Billy Crystal).

She was ready to retire from the TV business when her husband, TV producer Paul Junger Witt, brought home a new idea for a show about "older women in Miami" and she couldn't refuse. Not surprisingly, NBC had a slightly different idea of what "older" meant. Harris was thinking sixty-, seventy-, or eighty-year-old women, while the network had forty-year-olds in mind (her age at the time!). "We managed to compromise at the women hovering around late fifty, early sixties. But ultimately, their ages were never expressly mentioned," Harris said.

The show addressed age discrimination when Rose goes job hunting after her late husband's monthly pension is cut off. Blanche advises Rose to "dress youthful . . . Let's face it, honey, companies are not falling all over themselves to hire women your age." Rose soon finds out just how true that is. When she applies to be the assistant manager of a pet shop, she's told she's too old (even though she worked at a pet store in St. Olaf!).

Her pals give her a pep talk and a confidence booster, calling out the blatant age discrimination. "Rose, you can fight this," Blanche tells her. "You gotta stand up for your rights." All fired up and ready for action, Rose bursts into the local news station to report this job discrimination to the star consumer reporter, Enrique Mas (Chick Vennera). It turns out he's hiring a production assistant for his show. She's interested, but he says she's not the "right type. The job requires someone with great energy and drive and, quite frankly, someone of your advanced age . . ."

She interrupts him. "Wait a minute! I'm here on an age discrimination case, and you're telling me I'm too old!" Rose says. "You can't write me off just because I'm not thirtysomething. I have experience and wisdom and insight. I'd be perfect for this job." And what do you know, he gives her the job. Don't you love TV? And good friends who give you the strength to stand up for your rights!

The Golden Girls Keeps on Shining

The Golden Girls is the rare show that's only gained in popularity in the decades since it aired its last original episode. The show's audience continued to grow over time in syndication (starting in 1990), then on

Lifetime TV, introducing Rose Nylund and her hilarious housemates to a whole new generation of fans. By the summer of 2006—fifteen years after *The Golden Girls* ended its original run, the show was still drawing 11 million viewers per week and 30 million per month on Lifetime, where it had been airing since 1997. At times, the network would air *The Golden Girls* as many as seven times a day!

In 2017, Hulu nabbed the rights to stream the sassy sitcom. "*The Golden Girls* has really stood the test of time and is still resonating with audiences. So, when the opportunity came up to license it, we knew we had to take it," a Hulu spokesperson told CNBC. Hulu's gamble turned out to be a smart bet, with the cult '80s sitcom appealing to nostalgic viewers, particularly after the pandemic hit in March 2020. A *New York Times* story about what audiences watched early in the pandemic found, not surprisingly, that audiences sought out comfort viewing. In April 2020, Hulu viewers watched nearly 11 million hours of *The Golden Girls*. That's a lot of midnight cheesecake sessions! The show consistently ranked in Hulu's Top 10. If people couldn't see their real-life friends, they wanted to tune in to their old friends in Miami.

With the sustained interest in all things Betty and the devoted fan following of *The Golden Girls*, not surprisingly, there are countless fan accounts dedicated to the actress and the show on Instagram and other social media platforms. Fans have any number of Betty-bilia they can collect, including all sorts of merchandise, such as a Betty bobblehead, a Betty White Chia Pet, a Betty White prayer candle, coloring books, holiday ornaments, tiki glass, key chains, sweaters, mugs, and even social distancing masks. Now you can keep Betty close at all times!

You can buy *Golden Girls*–themed everything from Monopoly, Clue, and Trivial Pursuit to Pez dispensers, action figures, breakfast cereal, and, of course, cheesecake. During the pandemic, the video conferencing app Zoom created *Golden Girls* backgrounds so people could connect with their old Miami friends. Of course, there were lots of *Golden Girls* face masks!

In 2019, Disney ABC Television Group (which owns Hulu, which is streaming the show) proclaimed July 30 #GoldenGirlsDay! The date just so happens to also be National Cheesecake Day. How perfect is that?

Blanche's midcentury home at 6151 Richmond Street in Miami, Florida, went on the market in summer 2020. Except that's not a real address, and that's not where the show really filmed. For the first season of the show, the producers filmed the exterior of a midcentury house located in the tony Brentwood neighborhood of Los Angeles. In the following seasons, they filmed the facade of a replica of the house that was constructed on "Residential Street," a set at Disney-MGM Studios (now Disney's Hollywood Studios) in Orlando, Florida. It was a popular attraction on Disney's Backlot Tour for years, until 2014, when Disney shut down the Backlot Tour. Residential Street and all of the "homes" in the neighborhood, including *The Golden Girls*', were torn down.

Meanwhile, the original ranch house in Los Angeles where the first season was filmed ended up in a bidding war and sold for more than four million dollars—and no, cheesecake and wisecracks weren't included!

Who Said That:
Sue Ann, Rose, or Elka?

Betty helped create so many unforgettable characters through-out her epic career, but her three most famous TV roles are the ones fans quote the most:

Sue Ann Nivens, the over-the-top, backstabbing "Happy Homemaker" on *The Mary Tyler Moore Show*, the terminally naive **Rose Nylund** on *The Golden Girls*, and the blunt Polish grandmother with a colorful past **Elka Ostrovsky** on *Hot in Cleveland*. There's some overlap in their personalities, but they're distinctively different, too. Test your knowledge of their personalities through these snippets of dialogue below. Who said it?

1. "I wanted to be cremated and have my ashes thrown on Robert Redford."
   a. Elka Ostrovsky
   b. Rose Nylund
   c. Sue Ann Nivens

2. "The truth is I'm a great driver, but sometimes I like to drive real slow just to mess with people."
   a. Elka Ostrovsky
   b. Rose Nylund
   c. Sue Ann Nivens

3. "Who do you have to shag to get a drink around here?"
   a. Elka Ostrovsky
   b. Rose Nylund
   c. Sue Ann Nivens

4. "Just because it's my birthday, you don't have to go to all the trouble of going out and buying me a present. I'll do it for you!"
   a. Elka Ostrovsky
   b. Rose Nylund
   c. Sue Ann Nivens

5. "If the guy's a cutie, you've got to tap that bootie."
   a. Elka Ostrovsky
   b. Rose Nylund
   c. Sue Ann Nivens

6. "I'll be fine after a twenty-four-hour bender. Benders fix everything . . . except quitting alcohol."
   a. Elka Ostrovsky
   b. Rose Nylund
   c. Sue Ann Nivens

7. "I hate to admit it, but he melts my Häagen-Dazs."
   a. Elka Ostrovsky
   b. Rose Nylund
   c. Sue Ann Nivens

8. "Life is like a giant weenie roast, and I'm the biggest weenie."
   a. Elka Ostrovsky
   b. Rose Nylund
   c. Sue Ann Nivens

9. "Blow it out your Tubenburbles!"
   a. Elka Ostrovsky
   b. Rose Nylund
   c. Sue Ann Nivens

10. "I never thought I'd say this to a man, but get your hand off my knee!"
    a. Elka Ostrovsky
    b. Rose Nylund
    c. Sue Ann Nivens

11. "In my day, we didn't have therapy. We were too busy looking for food."
    a. Elka Ostrovsky
    b. Rose Nylund
    c. Sue Ann Nivens

12. "I do love telling people what they're doing wrong."
    a. Elka Ostrovsky
    b. Rose Nylund
    c. Sue Ann Nivens

13. "I was a child prodigy. I was reading cookbooks at two, and I started pickling at six. When I was twelve, I was quite heavily into sauces."
   a. Elka Ostrovsky
   b. Rose Nylund
   c. Sue Ann Nivens

14. "If you can't stand the heat, get out of my kitchen."
   a. Elka Ostrovsky
   b. Rose Nylund
   c. Sue Ann Nivens

15. "Please forgive me—it wasn't my fault. My cousins have been marrying each other for generations."
   a. Elka Ostrovsky
   b. Rose Nylund
   c. Sue Ann Nivens

Add up your responses.

If you got between 0–6 points: You've got some studying to do. You need to watch—or rewatch—*The Mary Tyler Moore Show* (you can start with season 4, since that's when Sue Ann arrives), *The Golden Girls*, and *Hot in Cleveland* pronto. Learn what makes Sue Ann, Rose, and Elka tick, and then take this quiz again.

If you got between 7–11 points: You're a respectable Betty White fan. Maybe you haven't seen every episode of these three series, but they clearly left an impression on you. Nice job!

If you got between 12–15 points: You're a true Betty White fan. You know and understand what motivates Sue Ann, Rose, and Elka. You can quote the best of Betty's lines from *The Mary Tyler Moore Show*, *The Golden Girls*, and even *Hot in Cleveland*. You're an honorary *Golden Girl*!

CHAPTER TEN

STAY GOLDEN!

IF YOU LIVE LONG ENOUGH IN HOLLYWOOD—
and are talented enough, and loved enough—you're bound to wind
up with a shelf full of trophies. Throughout her eighty-year-career,
White racked up the awards, including five Primetime Emmys and
one Daytime Emmy, plus two SAG Awards. Then there's the star on
the Hollywood Walk of Fame (next to her beloved Allen Ludden)
and the induction into the Television Academy Hall of Fame. Honestly,
there are too many to list here. One thing's for sure: Betty's certainly
never felt overlooked! "I got an award for everything," she told *Parade*.
"Inhaling, exhaling . . . I've been so spoiled rotten." Deservedly so, too!

In 2010, she was voted AP Entertainer of the year and was voted
the most trusted celebrity, according to a Reuters poll. Not content

with merely winning acting awards, she added a Grammy to her shelf in 2012, when she won Best Spoken Word Album for her reading of her book *If You Ask Me (And of Course You Won't)*. We're asking, Betty! What else, what else?

The following year, in March 2012, the still red-hot White was inducted to the NAB Broadcasting Hall of Fame. In his speech, NAB President and CEO Gordon Smith praised her "remarkable energy and an incredible ability to connect with viewers. Betty's contributions to television and entertainment as a whole are extraordinary. Our Hall of Fame would be incomplete without her."

At ninety-one, she was awarded the inaugural title of "Longest TV Career by an Entertainer (Female)" in the 2014 edition of the *Guinness Book of World Records* for her (then) seventy-four years in the business. (Previously, the category was nongender specific.) "I was astounded when they called to tell me," Betty said after hearing the news. "Who? Me!?! It's such an honor. I can't believe I'm now associated with it. I am amazed at some of the records they keep. The longest fingernails?!"

That same year, Betty's Q score—her "likability quotient"— ranked the highest in the industry, and she consistently tops the list of most popular and most trusted celebrities, according to a Reuters poll. Of course, talent alone isn't enough to make it in show business. People have to actually want to have you around. The people you work with have to enjoy your company. Over her many years in the notoriously cutthroat business, Betty is the rare celebrity who nobody seems to have anything bad to say about. Everyone who has worked with her has been struck by her modesty, generosity, sharp humor, and kindness. The audience admires her cheeky humor and indomitable spirit, too. In 2015, she was voted the People's Choice for Favorite TV Icon— at the age of ninety-three!

In 2018, celebrating her eightieth year in the entertainment industry, Betty was honored at the 70th Annual Emmy Awards for her many decades of contributions to the television industry. Remember: She was working in 1949, when the first Emmy ceremony was held; she was a nominee in the first-ever Best Actress category at the 3rd Primetime Emmy Awards in 1951. "There are very few people who were around then who are still working in television today. We are lucky to be joined by one of them, the greatest of all time, Betty White," said *SNL's* Kate McKinnon in introducing Betty.

Dressed in an elegant emerald sequined jacket, the radiant comedian walked onto the stage to the thunder of an enthusiastic standing ovation that took moments to die down. In her acceptance speech, she said that the first time she heard herself referred to as "the First Lady of Television," she took it as a compliment, until she heard the rest of the line . . . "She's that old, she was the first one way, way back when!" And, to be honest, she was.

> Some people like you, some don't. Now, I'm sure there's a world of people out there who can't stand me, but fortunately, there are enough people who do to keep me working.

Saying Goodbye

The hardest thing about growing old is having to say goodbye to friends, loved ones, and colleagues. "I always thought I would be the one who would go—particularly, with *The Golden Girls*, because I was the oldest. But then we lost all of them, and I'm the only one left and I'm still functioning. I think: How did that happen?" It would be easy to let all this loss get you down, yet Betty manages to absorb it and keep on smiling. After losing her parents and Allen, and then most of her friends and colleagues, Betty stayed busy and stayed positive. That's another reason we love her: She's a role model for all of us as we age. If we can be like Betty, getting old isn't so bad.

When asked how she'd like to be remembered after she's left us, Betty responded: "Warmly. I hope they remember something funny. I hope they remember a laugh." She's led an incredibly full life and, aside from wishing she'd married Ludden sooner, she has no regrets. "None. I consider myself to be the luckiest old broad on two feet," she said.

On her ninety-ninth birthday on January 17, 2021, the five-time Emmy Award winner expressed her thoughts on the momentous occasion: "I can stay up as late as I want without asking permission!" Meanwhile, her famous fans paid tribute to the Golden Girl. Country music legend Loretta Lynn, eighty-eight, tweeted: "Betty White is an American icon! I've always loved her. ninety-nine and doing fine—an inspiration to all us young girl(s). Thank you, Betty. I hope your birthday was fantastic and that this is your best year yet! We adore you. #wedontretire #firstladyoftv #rolemodel."

She received birthday wishes from her old colleague and friend Ed Asner, who said she's "a testament to living life on your own terms." Ellen DeGeneres called the Birthday Girl a "miracle in every way," and former president Bill Clinton tweeted: "Happy birthday, Betty White! You're a national treasure. Hillary and I hope you have a good one and wish you many, many more. With a little luck, we'll find a rerun of *Golden Girls* tonight!"

The birthday wishes kept coming with Craig Ferguson calling her "the sweetest, dearest, kindest, and funniest person I've ever had the good fortune to work with." *Mulan* actress Ming-Na Wen called White her "spirit animal" and a "queen" in her birthday tribute to White. Marie Osmond said White had taught her not to take herself "too seriously" and called the ninety-nine-year-old "99% pure perfection!"

Betty celebrated the special occasion quietly—and with a sense of humor, as usual: "What am I doing for my birthday? Running a mile each morning has been curtailed by COVID, so I am working on getting *The Pet Set* re-released and feeding the two ducks who come to visit me every day." We can only imagine that the Golden Girl is enjoying long conversations with her animal friends. Wouldn't you love to know what they're talking about?

How Well Do You Know Betty White's Career?

---

1. Betty worked with the father of which of the below actresses before they were born?
   - a. Sigourney Weaver
   - b. Meryl Streep
   - c. Goldie Hawn
   - d. Liza Minnelli

2. Betty played a sexy "biker chick" in skin-tight black leather on a 1978 episode of *The Carol Burnett Show* opposite which (then) young comedian?
   - a. Steve Martin
   - b. Richard Belzer
   - c. Freddie Prinze
   - d. Billy Crystal

3. Which show earned Betty her first Emmy?
   - a. *Hollywood on Television*
   - b. *Life with Elizabeth*
   - c. *The Betty White Show*
   - d. *The Mary Tyler Moore Show*

4. In 1987, Betty White had a cameo in which legal drama?
   a. *Law & Order*
   b. *Night Court*
   c. *Matlock*
   d. *L.A. Law*

5. In 2013, Betty played God in which comedy series?
   a. *Brooklyn Nine-Nine*
   b. *Getting On*
   c. *Mom*
   d. *Save Me*

6. Betty is credited on IMDb for creating one TV series. Which was it?
   a. *Life with Elizabeth*
   b. *The Betty White Show*
   c. *The Mary Tyler Moore Show*
   d. *The Pet Set*

7. In 2006, Betty cracked jokes at Comedy Central's Roast of this actor:
   a. Bob Newhart
   b. William Shatner
   c. Patrick Stewart
   d. Morgan Freeman

8. After appearing in the film *Advise & Consent* in 1962,
Betty didn't appear on the big screen again for how many years:

    a. 5 years

    b. 12 years

    c. 26 years

    d. 36 years

9. In 2008, Betty provided the voice of a grandma named
Yoshie in which acclaimed animated Japanese film?

    a. *Ponyo*

    b. *My Neighbor Totoro*

    c. *Howl's Moving Castle*

    d. *Spirited Away*

10. In 1988, Betty appeared with friends and fellow celebrity
contestants Lucille Ball and Carol Channing in a special charity
episode of which game show:

    a. *The Price Is Right*

    b. *Jeopardy!*

    c. *Let's Make a Deal*

    d. *Super Password*

11. From 1977 to 1978, Betty played the character of TV actress
Joyce Whitman on which series?

    a. *The Joyce Whitman Show*

    b. *The Betty White Show*

    c. *The Mary Tyler Moore Show*

    d. *The Carol Burnett Show*

12. Starting in season 4 of *The Mary Tyler Moore Show*, from 1973 to 1977, Betty White played the "Happy Homemaker" Sue Ann Nivens in how many episodes?

    a. 45 episodes

    b. 15 episodes

    c. 30 episodes

    d. 60 episodes

13. Betty played a Macy's Parade hostess in an episode of which popular '80s TV series?

    a. *Hotel*

    b. *The Love Boat*

    c. *Who's the Boss?*

    d. *Alf*

14. Though she's not a fan of reality TV, Betty appeared as herself in an episode of which reality TV series?

    a. *The Real Housewives of Orange County*

    b. *The Real Housewives of Beverly Hills*

    c. *MasterChef*

    d. *Storage Wars*

15. Betty's won more awards than we can keep track of. Which of the below awards has Betty White *not* won?

    a. Primetime Emmy Award

    b. Daytime Emmy Award

    c. Grammy Award

    d. Golden Globe Award

A. **EXTRA CREDIT** (worth 2 points each): Betty played Vicki Angel on the early, short-lived sitcom *A Date with the Angels*, which was loosely based on a play by Pulitzer Prize–winning playwright Elmer Rice. What was the name of the play?

    a. *Dream Girl*

    b. *The Adding Machine*

    c. *The Left Bank*

    d. *A New Life*

B. **DOUBLE EXTRA CREDIT** (worth 4 points!): Betty starred alongside Donna Reed, Gloria Stuart, and Timothy Hutton in which 1979 TV miniseries?

    a. *The Miracle Worker*

    b. *The Berenstain Bear's Christmas Tree*

    c. *The Best Place to Be*

    d. *Same Time Next Year*

Add up your responses. For each correct answer, you get 1 point. If you get the EXTRA CREDIT question correct, you get 2 points. If you get the DOUBLE EXTRA CREDIT correct, you get 4 points (so the most number of points you can get is 19).

If you got between 0–6 points: Frankly, we're disappointed. You could do better. Betty deserves better! Your assignment is to read Betty White's memoirs, starting with *In Person*, which was first published in 1987. Study up and show respect to the Goldenest Girl.

If you got between 7–12 points: Not bad. We're mildly impressed. You know your Betty White career facts. Still, you might want to read her memoir *Here We Go Again*, first published in 1995. You could learn a lot from the legend!

If you got between 13–18 points: Wow. You are a true Betty White expert. You've followed her career and pay her the utmost respect by remembering her many roles. Still, you should go refresh your memory by binge-watching *The Golden Girls*.

If you got 19 points: We're not worthy! Seriously, you probably know Betty White's career better than she does. Maybe you should write your own Betty White book!

ACKNOWLEDGMENTS

This book wouldn't exist without Betty White, whose amazing life and career helped buoy me when the future felt more uncertain than ever. I feel enormously lucky to have the opportunity to devote time to someone as quintessentially hopeful and undeniably inspirational as Ms. White. Thanks to my agent Peter Steinberg, my editor Jennifer Kasius, the team at Running Press for helping to make this book a reality, and to Jess Riordan for guiding it to the finish line.

I'm indebted to the many authors, writers, and podcasters whose interviews and writings helped me to better understand the great lady herself. I've credited my sources in the Bibliography, but there are a few that proved especially invaluable. In particular, I appreciate author Jim Colucci's passion and dedication to all things *Golden Girls*. His books, including *The Q Guide to The Golden Girls* and *Golden Girls Forever: An Unauthorized Look Behind the Lanai* provided keen insight into that classic show. I drew inspiration from Jennifer Keishin Armstrong's excellent *Mary and Lou and Rhoda and Ted: And All the Brilliant Minds Who Made The Mary Tyler Moore Show A Classic*. I also relied on the extensive research that author Kliph Nesteroff undertook into Betty White's early career, as well as interviews conducted by The Paley Center for Media, the Television Academy Foundation, and the team behind PBS's *Betty White: First Lady of Television*.

Finally, thanks to my parents, Bernard and Marilyn Bernstein, for supporting my writing dreams and for letting me watch as much TV as I wanted, and to my husband, Anthony, for being a true partner in life. I couldn't have done it without you!

BIBLIOGRAPHY

Alda, Alan, interviewer. "Betty White and Alan Alda Fall Desperately in Love." *Clear+Vivid with Alan Alda*, March 23, 2020. Podcast, 38:18. https://podcasts.apple.com/us/podcast/betty-white-and-alan-alda-fall-desperately-in-love/id1400082430?i=1000469293354.

Alley, Robert S. and Irby B. Brown. *Love Is All Around: The Making of The Mary Tyler Moore Show*. New York: Delta, 1989.

Artisan News Service. "Betty White Turns 90, Old and New Hollywood Celebrates." January 13, 2012. Video, 3:04. https://www.youtube.com/watch?v=xCseAENCyE4.

Associated Press. "Want TV Ratings? Hire Betty White, CBS Finds." CBSNews.com. February 1, 2011. Accessed March 29, 2021. https://www.cbsnews.com/news/want-tv-ratings-hire-betty-white-cbs-finds/.

Baez, Christina. "14 Times Betty White's Fashion Choices Were Hot as Hell." *Us Weekly* (January 17, 2020). Accessed March 27, 2021. https://www.usmagazine.com/stylish/pictures/betty-whites-best-sexy-style-and-fashion-moments/.

Bevil, Dewayne. "Disney's Studio Backlot Tour Turning Out the Lights." *Orlando Sentinel*, September 26, 2014. Accessed March 27, 2021. https://www.orlandosentinel.com/travel/attractions/the-daily-disney/os-disney-hollywood-studios-backlot-tour-20140925-story.html.

Bilger, Audrey. "Betty White Isn't a Feminist, But . . ." *Ms.* (May 2, 2011). Accessed March 11, 2021. https://msmagazine.com/2011/05/02/betty-white-isnt-a-feminist-but/.

Boettcher, Steve, dir. *Betty White: First Lady of Television*. Aired August 21, 2018, on PBS. https://www.netflix.com/title/81173792.

Bravo, Tony. "Why 'The Golden Girls' Continues to Resonate with Us Three Decades Later." Datebook.SFChronicle.com. Updated December 18, 2020. Accessed March 29, 2021. https://datebook.sfchronicle.com/movies-tv/why-the-golden-girls-continues-to-resonate-with-us-three-decades-later.

Braxton, Greg. "Q&A; with Bob Newhart and Betty White: Old 'Bob,' New Angle, New Friends." *Los Angeles Times*, October 21, 1993. Accessed March 27, 2021. https://www.latimes.com/archives/la-xpm-1993-10-21-ca-48158-story.html.

Bruni, Frank, interviewer. "A Conversation with Betty White" on *TimesTalks*. *New York Times* Events, October 18, 2012. Video, 5:07. https://www.youtube.com/watch?v=3LNjmo4Cbaw.

—. "Facing Age with a Saucy Wink." *New York Times*, April 28, 2011. Accessed March 19, 2021. https://www.nytimes.com/2011/05/01/arts/television/betty-whites-post-80-career-high.html.

Brunner, Jeryl. "23 Betty White Quotes that Make Us Love Her Even More." *Parade* (January 17, 2021). Accessed March 29, 2021. https://parade.com/451087/jerylbrunner/15-quotes-that-make-us-love-betty-white/.

Bullock Sandra, Ryan Reynolds, and Betty White. "Sandra Bullock & Ryan Reynolds: Behind the Scenes of *The Proposal*." FunnyorDie.com. May 15, 2009. Video, 3:51. Accessed March 27, 2021. https://www.funnyordie.com/2009/5/15/18187439/sandra-bullock-ryan-reynolds-behind-the-scenes-of-the-proposal.

Bukszpan, Daniel. "Why Hulu Is Hoping to Turn Old 'Golden Girls' episodes into Mine." CNBC.com. Updated January 30, 2017. Accessed March 29, 2021. https://www.cnbc.com/2017/01/27/why-hulu-is-hoping-to-turn-old-golden-girls-episodes-into-a-goldmine.html.

Cadiff, Andy, dir. *Hot in Cleveland*. Season 2, episode 5, "I Love Lucci: Part One." Aired February 16, 2011, on TV Land.

—. *Hot in Cleveland*. Season 2, episode 6, "I Love Lucci: Part Two." Aired February 23, 2011, on TV Land.

—. *Hot in Cleveland*. Season 2, episode 20, "Indecent Proposals." Aired August 17, 2011, on TV Land.

—. *Hot in Cleveland*. Season 4, episode 23, "Love Is All Around." Aired September 4, 2013, on TV Land.

—. *Hot in Cleveland*. Season 5, episode 9, "Bad George Clooney." Aired June 4, 2014, on TV Land.

—. *Hot in Cleveland*. Season 5, episode 22, "Win Win." Aired August 27, 2014, on TV Land.

Campaign US. "Case Study: How Fame Made Snickers' 'You're Not You When You're Hungry' Campaign a Success." CampaignLive.com. October 26, 2016. Accessed March 27, 2021. https://www.campaignlive.com/article/case-study-fame-made-snickers-youre-not-when-youre-hungry-campaign-success/1413554.

Cancian, Dan. "Betty White Fans Flood Twitter as Actress Turns 99, Says Will Be 'Up as Late as I Want.'" *Newsweek* (January 17, 2021). Accessed March 29, 2021. https://www.newsweek.com/betty-white-fans-twitter-actress-turns-99-says-late-1562216#.

Chestang, Raphael. "Betty White Is Still Living Life on Her Own Terms as She Turns 93." ETOnline.com. January 16, 2015. Accessed March 12, 2021. https://www.etonline.com/news/156433_betty_white_is_still_living_life_on_her_own_terms_as_she_turns_93.

Colucci, Jim. Golden Girls *Forever: An Unauthorized Look Behind the Lanai*. New York: Harper Design, 2016.

—. *The Q Guide to* The Golden Girls. New York: Alyson Books, 2006.

Cooper, Anderson, interviewer. Betty White interview on *Anderson Live*. Aired December 5, 2011, on CNN.

DeGeneres, Ellen, interviewer. Betty White interview on *The Ellen DeGeneres Show*. Aired October 11, 2010, on NBC.

Diamond, Matthew, dir. *The Golden Girls*. Season 6, episode 10, "Girls Just Wanna Have Fun . . . Before They Die." Aired November 24, 1990, on NBC.

—. *The Golden Girls*. Season 6, episode 11, "Stand by Your Man." Aired December 1, 1990, on NBC.

—. *The Golden Girls*. Season 6, episode 14, "Sister of the Bride." Aired January 12, 1991, on NBC.

Dogs for the Blind. "Betty White Supports Guide Dogs for the Blind." PSA, January 23, 2013.

The Early Show interview with Betty White (*The Proposal*). Aired June 12, 2009, on CBS. https://www.youtube.com/watch?v=ondVWfAuHCg.

Fallon, Kevin. "Betty White on Surviving 63 Years in Show Business with No Backbone." *The Atlantic* (May 11, 2011). Accessed March 27, 2021. https://www.theatlantic.com/entertainment/archive/2011/05/betty-white-on-surviving-63-years-in-show-business-with-no-backbone/238752/.

Fantozzi, Tony, interviewer. Interview with Betty White in Los Angeles, CA, Television Academy Foundation, June 4, 1997. Video, 23:44. https://interviews.televisionacademy.com/interviews/betty-white.

Fitzharris, Dustin. "Catching Up with *The Golden Girls'* Susan Harris." *Out* (October 3, 2010). Accessed March 26, 2021. https://www.out.com/entertainment/television/2010/10/03/catching-golden-girls-susan-harris.

Fletcher, Anne, dir. *The Proposal*. Touchstone Pictures, 2009.

Foley, Kaye. "Betty White on Her 95th Birthday." Katie Couric, Global Anchor. Yahoo! News, January 17, 2017. Accessed March 19, 2021. https://news.yahoo.com/betty-white-on-her-95th-birthday-095426492.html.

Gambino, Megan. "Betty White on Her Love for Animals." *Smithsonian* (May 14, 2012). Accessed March 19, 2021. https://www.smithsonianmag.com/science-nature/betty-white-on-her-love-for-animals-92610121/.

Ganss, Will. "'Golden Girls' Facts that May Surprise Even the Biggest Fans." GoodMorningAmerica.com. July 30, 2019. Accessed March 29, 2021. https://www.goodmorningamerica.com/culture/story/golden-girls-facts-surprise-biggest-fans-56810093.

Gilbert, Matthew. "White Plays It Straight in Syrupy 'Valentine.'" *Boston Globe*, January 28, 2011. Accessed March 29, 2021. http://archive.boston.com/ae/tv/articles/2011/01/28/white_plays_it_straight_in_syrupy_lost_valentine/.

Gould, Jack. "Television in Review; Betty White's Comic Antics Deserving of Better Spot." *New York Times*, March 24, 1954. Accessed March 11, 2021. https://www.nytimes.com/1954/03/24/archives/television-in-review-betty-whites-comic-antics-deserving-of-better.html.

Graham, Lauren. *Talking as Fast as I Can: From* Gilmore Girls *to* Gilmore Girls *(and Everything in Between)*. New York: Ballantine Books, 2016.

Grosvenor, Carrie. "Betty White: First Lady of Game Shows." LiveAbout.com. Updated April 16, 2018. Accessed March 31, 2021. https://www.liveabout.com/ betty-white-game-shows-host-1396519.

Hafner, Josh. "The Funniest Super Bowl Ads of All Time: Betty White, Terry Tate and Avocados." *USA Today*, January 22, 2018. Accessed March 27, 2021. https://www.usatoday.com/story/money/nation-now/2018/01/22/funniest-super-bowl-ads-all-time-betty-white-terry-tate-and-avocados/1055407001/.

Hajek, Danny. "Betty White, The Golden Girl from the Golden Days of Television." "My Big Break" audio series on *All Things Considered*, NPR, November 2, 2014. https://www.npr.org/2014/11/02/360425512/betty-white-the-golden-girl-from-the-golden-days-of-television.

Harrison, Cameron and Angeline Jane Bernabe. "Alex Trebek Reveals Who He Wants to Replace Him as the Host of 'Jeopardy!'" GoodMorningAmerica.com, July 21, 2020. Accessed March 11, 2021. https://www.goodmorningamerica.com/culture/story/ alex-trebek-reveals-replace-host-jeopardy-71889573.

Havel, Carrie, associate dir. *Little Big Shots: Forever Young*. Season 1, episode 1, "Forever Young." Aired June 21, 2017, on NBC.

Haven, Riley. "Betty White Talks Reading, Game Shows and Her Celebrity Crush." *Parade* (August 20, 2018). Accessed March 13, 2021. https://parade.com/694313/rielyhaven/ exclusive-interview-betty-white-talks-reading-game-shows-and-her-celebrity-crush/.

Herbert, Steven. "'Golden' Shades of White." *Los Angeles Times*, September 13, 1992. Accessed March 19, 2021. https://www.latimes.com/archives/la-xpm-1992-09-13-tv-1139-story.html.

Hewitt, Bill and the editors of *Life*. *Life Icons: Betty White: The Illustrated Biography*. New York: Life Books, 2012.

Hollow, Michele C. "Betty White Dishes on Her 'Very Expensive Habit.'" *Parade* (August 5, 2013). Accessed March 19, 2021. https://parade.com/ 53369/michelechollow/betty-white-dishes-on-her-love-of-animals/.

Holmes, Linda. "This Time, Facebook Is Right: Betty White Should Host 'Saturday Night Live.'" NPR.org, February 11, 2010. Accessed March 11, 2021. https://www.npr.org/2010/02/11/114524455/this-time-facebook-is-right-betty-white-should-host-saturday-night-live.

Hughes, Terry, dir. *The Golden Girls*. Season 1, episode 15, "In a Bed of Rose's." Aired January 11, 1986, on NBC.

—. *The Golden Girls*. Season 1, episode 17, "Nice and Easy." Aired February 1, 1986, on NBC.

—. *The Golden Girls*. Season 1, episode 25, "The Way We Met." Aired May 10, 1986, on NBC.

—. *The Golden Girls*. Season 2, episode 4, "It's a Miserable Life." Aired November 1, 1986, on NBC.

—. *The Golden Girls*. Season 2, episode 5, "Isn't It Romantic?" Aired November 8, 1986, on NBC.

—. *The Golden Girls*. Season 2, episode 11, "'Twas the Nightmare Before Christmas." Aired December 20, 1986, on NBC.

—. *The Golden Girls*. Season 3, episode 3, "Bringing Up Baby." Aired October 3, 1987, on NBC.

—. *The Golden Girls*. Season 3, episode 11, "Three on a Couch." Aired December 5, 1987, on NBC.

—. *The Golden Girls*. Season 3, episode 23, "Mixed Blessings." Aired March 19, 1988, on NBC.

—. *The Golden Girls*. Season 4, episode 1, "Yes, We Have No Havanas." Aired October 8, 1988, on NBC.

—. *The Golden Girls*. Season 5, episode 4, "Rose Fights Back." Aired October 21, 1989, on NBC.

—. *The Golden Girls*. Season 5, episode 19, "72 Hours." Aired February 17, 1990, on NBC.

Huguenin, Patrick. "Betty White Still a Scene Stealer in 'The Proposal' alongside Sandra Bullock and Ryan Reynolds. *New York Daily News*, June 16, 2009. Accessed March 27, 2021. https://www.nydailynews.com/entertainment/tv-movies/betty-white-scene-stealer-proposal-sandra-bullock-ryan-reynolds-article-1.375226.

Hunt, Stacey Wilson. "*The Golden Girls* Creators on Finding a New Generation of Fans and Giving George Clooney One of His Earliest Jobs." Vulture.com (March 3, 2017). Accessed March 27, 2021. https://www.vulture.com/2017/03/the-golden-girls-creators-on-finding-new-fans.html.

Itzkoff, Dave. "Betty White Helps Boost Ratings of 'SNL.'" *New York Times*, May 9, 2010. Accessed March 27, 2021. https://www.nytimes.com/2010/05/10/arts/television/10arts-BETTYWHITEHE_BRF.html.

—. "It's Friday, So Why Not Talk to Betty White?" *New York Times*, August 6, 2010. Accessed March 29, 2021. https://artsbeat.blogs.nytimes.com/2010/08/06/its-friday-so-why-not-talk-to-betty-white/.

James, Susan Donaldson. "Betty White, Nearly 90, Fights Old-Age Stereotypes for AARP." ABCNews.go.com. May 23, 2011. Accessed March 29, 2021. https://abcnews.go.com/Health/actress-betty-white-fights-age-stereotypes-aarp/story?id=13667587.

Janela, Mike. "Q-and-A: Betty White on Her World Record, Her Favorite Works, and Getting Started on TV." GuinnessWorldRecords.com. September 4, 2013. Accessed March 29, 2021. https://www.guinnessworldrecords.com/news/2013/9/q-and-a-betty-white-on-her-world-record-her-favorite-works-and-getting-started-on-tv-50966/?fb_comment_id=663687296977673_7796233.

Justin, Neal. "Betty White Not Afraid to Show Her Bawdy Side." *Chicago Tribune*, May 5, 2010. Accessed March 27, 2021. https://www.chicagotribune.com/entertainment/ct-xpm-2010-05-05-sc-ent-0503-tvcolumn-wed-20100505-story.html.

Keveney, Bill. "Betty White's Legendary Cake-Riding Skills, as Told by Her 'MTM' Co-Star Gavin MacLeod." *USA Today*, updated on August 1, 2018. Accessed March 19, 2021. https://www.usatoday.com/story/life/tv/2018/07/31/mary-tyler-moore-co-star-marvels-betty-whites-cake-riding-skills/874733002/.

—. "Betty White Says Goodbye to 'Cleveland.'" *USA Today*, June 2, 2015. Accessed March 29, 2021. https://www.usatoday.com/story/life/tv/2015/06/02/betty-white-talks-hot-in-cleveland-career-and-friendship/28317461/.

King, Don Roy, dir. *Saturday Night Live*. Season 35, episode 21: "Betty White/Jay-Z." Aired May 8, 2010, on NBC.

King, Larry, interviewer. Betty White interview on *Larry King Now*.
Aired April 22, 2014, on Ora TV.

Kline, Robert, dir. *Betty White Champion for Animals*. Amazon Prime Video, 2012.

Koblin, John. "Lockdown TV: Netflix Dominates, News Surges and Bea Arthur
is Still Golden." *New York Times*, April 30, 2020. Accessed March 29, 2021.
https://www.nytimes.com/2020/04/30/business/media/coronavirus-television-
netflix-ratings.html#.

Kotkin, Joel. "The Bitter End of 'Betty White.'" *Washington Post*, January 9, 1978.
Accessed March 19, 2021. https://www.washingtonpost.com/archive/lifestyle/
1978/01/09/the-bitter-end-of-betty-white/fe142bca-54ae-4553-9636-367eba04bb1a/.

Kubey, Robert. *Creating Television: Conversations with the People Behind 50 Years of American TV*.
Mahwah, NJ: Lawrence Erlbaum Associates, Inc., 2004.

Letterman, David, interviewer. Betty White on *Late Night with David Letterman*.
Aired October 1, 1985, on NBC.

Littleton, Cynthia. "Betty White on Her 70 Years in TV: 'The Word 'No' Did Not Exist.'"
Variety (September 17, 2020). Accessed March 11, 2021.
https://variety.com/2020/tv/news/emmy-winner-betty-white-1234772136/.

Lopez, George, interviewer. Betty White on *Lopez Tonight*. Aired January 20, 2010, on TBS.

Mabrey, Vicki and Eric Johnson. "Betty White's Wild Kingdom."
ABCNews.go.com, June 11, 2010. Accessed March 19, 2021.
https://abcnews.go.com/Nightline/betty-white-nightline/story?id=10886536.

MacNicol, Peter, dir. *Ally McBeal*. Season 3, episode 3, "Seeing Green."
Aired November 8, 1999, on Fox.

Margulies, Lee. "NBC Starts Fast in Ratings Race." *Los Angeles Times*,
September 18, 1985. Accessed March 19, 2021. https://www.latimes.com/
archives/la-xpm-1985-09-18-ca-6290-story.html.

McDermott, Maeve. "Betty White Dramatically Reads Queen Latifah Lyrics at VH1 Hip Hop Honors." *USA Today*, July 12, 2016. Video, 0:28. Accessed March 29, 2021. https://www.usatoday.com/story/life/entertainthis/2016/07/12/betty-white-queen-latifah-lyrics-vh1-hip-hop-honors-michelle-obama/86980918/.

McDowell, Jeanne Dorin. "What Women Want: Kristen Bell, Jamie Lee Curtis, and Betty White on Sex, Love, and . . . Staying Hot!" AARP.org, September 13, 2010. Accessed March 13, 2021. https://www.aarp.org/entertainment/movies-tv/info-09-2010/what_women_want.html.

McGovern, Joe. "How Four Comedy Legends Were Cast in *Toy Story 4*." *Entertainment Weekly* (June 28, 2019). Accessed March 27, 2021. https://ew.com/movies/2019/06/28/comedy-legends-toy-story-4/.

Milliner, Todd. "*Hot in Cleveland* Producer Recalls That *Mary Tyler Moore* Reunion Episode." *Entertainment Weekly* (January 26, 2017). Accessed March 29, 2021. https://ew.com/tv/2017/01/26/hot-in-cleveland-mary-tyler-moore-reunion-producer-guest-column/.

Miner, Steve, dir. *Lake Placid*. 20th Century Fox, 1999.

Moore, Steven Dean, dir. *The Simpsons*. Season 11, episode 15, "Missionary: Impossible." Aired February 20, 2000, on Fox.

Moradel, Joshua. "These Are Betty White's Tips for Living a Long and Happy Life, and She Is REALLY the Best." BuzzFeed.com. January 17, 2019. Accessed March 29, 2021. https://www.buzzfeed.com/joshuagmoradel/betty-white-age-birthday-97-tips-for-living.

Morris Animal Foundation. "Betty White Fund Helps Rare Antelope in Crisis." MorrisAnimalFoundation.org, November 11, 2010. Accessed March 19, 2021. https://www.morrisanimalfoundation.org/article/betty-white-fund-helps-rare-antelope-crisis#.

Morrison, Mark. "Laughter's Leading Ladies: Betty White and Mindy Kaling Compare Notes on Eight Decades of Funny Business." *Emmy* (March 10, 2016). Accessed March 11, 2021. https://www.emmys.com/news/features/laughters-leading-ladies.

Morgan, Piers, interviewer. Betty White on *Piers Morgan Tonight*. Aired April 17, 2012, on CNN.

MPI Media Group. "Betty White's Pet Set: A TV Icon's Show Returns After 50 Years." PRNewswire, Dec. 17, 2020. Accessed March 11, 2021. https://www.prnewswire.com/news-releases/betty-whites-pet-set-a-tv-icons-show-returns-after-50-years-301195464.html.

Mulkerrins, Jane. "The Golden Age of Betty White: At 89 with a New Show and an Eye for the Boys, This Golden Girl's Far from Retiring." *Daily Mail*, April 7, 2011. Accessed March 29, 2021. https://www.dailymail.co.uk/tvshowbiz/article-1374592/Golden-Girl-Betty-White-89-new-eye-boys.html.

Murrian, Samuel R. "Betty White on Her Legacy, Memories and Her Recipe for Living a Long, Happy Life." *Parade* (January 5, 2018). Accessed March 11, 2021. https://parade.com/634316/samuelmurrian/betty-white-on-her-legacy-memories-and-her-recipe-for-living-a-long-happy-life/.

National Association of Broadcasters. "Renowned Actress Betty White to Be Inducted into NAB Broadcasting Hall of Fame." NAB.org. March 16, 2012. Accessed March 29, 2021. https://www.nab.org/documents/newsRoom/pressRelease.asp?id=2708.

National Greyhound Adoption program website. https://www.ngap.org/betty-whites-greyhound-connection-y573.html.

Nedeff, Adam. *The Life (and Wife) of Allen Ludden*. Albany, GA: BearManor Media, 2017.

Nesteroff, Kliph. "The Early Betty White 1947–1973." *WFMU's Beware of the Blog* (blog), April 4, 2010. https://blog.wfmu.org/freeform/2010/04/the-early-betty-white.html.

Ng, Philiana. "'Hot in Cleveland' Creator on Show Secrets, Eve of 'Betty White Fever' and Ultimate Dream Cameo." *Hollywood Reporter* (August 27, 2014). Accessed March 27, 2021. https://www.hollywoodreporter.com/news/hot-cleveland-creator-show-secrets-726111.

Oprah.com. "The Unstoppable Betty White." Oprah.com. April 6, 2010. Accessed March 27, 2021. https://www.oprah.com/oprahshow/betty-whites-big-comeback/all.

The Paley Center for Media. *The Golden Girls* at PaleyFest LA 2006: Full Conversation in Los Angeles, CA. March 10, 2006. Video, 1:15. https://www.youtube.com/watch?v=W5z9zHcgQSg.

Parade. "Betty White Reacts to Robert Pattinson's 'Sexy' Comment." *Parade* (March 3, 2010).
Accessed March 29, 2021. https://parade.com/95086/parade/betty-white-reacts-to-robert-pattinsons-sexy-comment/.

Paskin, Willa. "Is It Now Illegal to Criticize Betty White?"
Vulture.com. June 16, 2010. Accessed March 29, 2021.
https://www.vulture.com/2010/06/will_it_ever_be_okay_to_critci.html#.

Passaris, Lex, dir. *The Golden Girls*. Season 7, episode 3, "Beauty and the Beast."
Aired October 5, 1991, on NBC.

—. *The Golden Girls*. Season 7, episode 8, "The Monkey Show."
Aired November 9, 1991, on NBC.

—. *The Golden Girls*. Season 7, episode 23, "One Flew Out of the Cuckoo's Nest."
Aired May 9, 1992, on NBC.

—. *The Golden Palace*. Season 1, episode 19, "A New Leash on Life."
Aired April 2, 1993, on CBS.

Patten, Dominic. "The Betty White Phenomenon: Why Her, Why Now?" TheWrap.com.
Updated May 17, 2010. Accessed March 27, 2021. https://www.thewrap.com/betty-white-phenomenon-why-her-why-now-17345/.

People.com. "Video: See Betty White and Aubrey Plaza as a Grandmother and a Goth
in *SpongeBob SquarePants*!" People.com, March 9, 2016. Accessed March 27, 2021.
https://people.com/tv/spongebob-squarepants-see-betty-white-and-aubrey-plaza/.

Pioneers of Television. "Betty White on the Early Days of TV." PBS.org, January 3, 2011.
Video, 0:23. https://www.pbs.org/video/pioneers-of-television-betty-white-on-the-early-days-of-tv/.

Powell, John and Cinco Paul. "Let It Grow." *Dr. Seuss' The Lorax—Original Songs
from the Motion Picture*. Universal Pictures/Interscope Records, 2012.

Rafkin, Alan, dir. *The Mary Tyler Moore Show*. Season 5, episode 10, "What Are Friends For?"
Aired November 16, 1974, on CBS.

Reese, Diana. "Bradley Bell Teases the Future of *The Bold and the Beautiful* and Says Social Issues Will Remain Key Storylines." *Parade* (March 19, 2019). Accessed March 27, 2021. https://parade.com/862157/dianareese/bradley-bell-teases-the-future-of-the-bold-and-the-beautiful-and-says-social-issues-will-remain-key-storylines/.

Reimel, Erin and Krystin Arneson. "Hollywood Celebrities on Being Child-Free by Choice." *Glamour* (March 17, 2019). Accessed March 13, 2021. https://www.glamour.com/gallery/hollywood-celebrities-on-being-child-free-by-choice.

Roffman, Marisa. "Betty White Gives a Sparkle to 'SpongeBob SquarePants.'" TVInsider.com, February 25, 2016. Accessed March 27, 2021. https://www.tvinsider.com/74707/betty-white-visits-spongebob-squarepants-photo/.

Rothenberg, Fred. "Humorous Homage to *Moore Show*." *Los Angeles Times*, Nov. 27, 1985. Accessed March 27, 2021. https://www.latimes.com/archives/la-xpm-1985-11-27-ca-4706-story.html.

Ryan, Patrick. "'Golden Girls' at 35: 5 Ways the Classic Sitcom Was Way Ahead of Its Time." *USA Today*, September 14, 2020. Accessed March 29, 2021. https://www.usatoday.com/story/entertainment/tv/2020/09/14/golden-girls-35th-anniversary-sitcom-groundbreaking-betty-white/5790843002/.

Sandrich, Jay, dir. *The Mary Tyler Moore Show*. Season 4, episode 1, "The Lars Affair." Aired September 15, 1973, on CBS.

—. *The Mary Tyler Moore Show*. Season 5, episode 7, "A New Sue Ann." Aired October 26, 1974, on CBS.

—. *The Mary Tyler Moore Show*. Season 6, episode 18, "Once I Had a Secret Love." Aired January 17, 1976, on CBS.

—. *The Mary Tyler Moore Show*. Season 7, episode 3, "Sue Ann's Sister." Aired October 9, 1976, on CBS.

Scardino, Don, dir. *30 Rock*. Season 4, episode 3, "Stone Mountain." Aired October 29, 2009, on NBC.

Scott, Vernon. "Betty White Just Right for 'Just Men,'" United Press International, March 7, 1983. https://www.upi.com/Archives/1983/03/07/Scotts-WorldNEWLNBetty-White-just-right-for-Just-Men/6198415861200/.

TheSevenSees.com. "*Dr. Seuss' The Lorax*—Betty White Talks about Doing Voice-Over Work." February 29, 2012. Video, 0:37. https://www.youtube.com/watch?v=-oe_25VVMFw.

"70th Emmy Awards: A Celebration for Betty White." September 17, 2018. Video, 5:00. https://www.emmys.com/video/70th-emmy-awards-celebration-betty-white.

Shales, Tom, "'Just Men' Is Unjust to All." *The Washington Post*, January 4, 1983. https://www.washingtonpost.com/archive/lifestyle/1983/01/04/just-men-is-unjust-to-all/76622fb9-b368-445d-804e-e3cca6f05176/.

Sherwood, Mary, co-producer. The Golden Girls: *Their Greatest Moments*. Aired June 2, 2003, on Lifetime.

Shira, Dahvi. "Betty White Jokes: I'm 'Much Sexier' at 91 Years Old Than I Was at 90." *People* (February 5, 2013). Accessed March 29, 2021. https://people.com/tv/betty-white-jokes-im-much-sexier-at-91-years-old-than-i-was-at-90/.

16th Annual Screen Actors Guild Awards. Aired January 23, 2010, on TNT and TBS.

Smitek, Colleen. "Hot Shots: Betty White." *Cleveland Magazine* (December 17, 2010). Accessed March 11, 2021. https://clevelandmagazine.com/entertainment/film-tv/articles/hot-shots-betty-white.

Spiller, Michael, dir. *Ugly Betty*. Season 2, episode 10, "Bananas for Betty." Aired December 6, 2007, on ABC.

Stanley, Alessandra. "Stay. Eat. Make Yourself at Home. Maybe Find a Man." *New York Times*, June 15, 2010. Accessed March 27, 2021. https://www.nytimes.com/2010/06/16/arts/television/16hot.html.

Stanley, T. L. "Betty White's Golden Touch Keeps Her Red-Hot." *Los Angeles Times*, April 12, 2010. Accessed March 27, 2021. https://www.latimes.com/archives/la-xpm-2010-apr-12-la-et-betty-white12-2010apr12-story.html.

Starr, Michael. "Betty White Has a Surprising Celebrity Crush." *New York Post*, August 10, 2018. Accessed March 19, 2021. https://nypost.com/2018/08/10/betty-white-has-a-surprising-celebrity-crush/.

Sternbergh, Adam. "2. But Stick with What Works." *New York* (May 14, 2010). Accessed March 19, 2021. https://nymag.com/arts/tv/goodtvguide/66067/.

Sutton, Samantha. "*The Golden Girls* Are Still the Best-Dressed TV Characters in History." *In Style* (February 3, 2020). Accessed March 26, 2021. https://www.instyle.com/fashion/golden-girls-tv-show-fashion-best-outfits.

Thompson, Kyra, interviewer. "Comedian Betty White on Carol Burnett." *American Masters Podcast*. Interview was for *Carol Burnett: A Woman of Character* (2007). Podcast, 22:20. https://www.pbs.org/wnet/americanmasters/podcast/betty-white-carol-burnett/.

Thrasher, Steven W. "The Real Mud on *The Golden Girls*." Vulture.com (July 2, 2020). Accessed March 26, 2021. https://www.vulture.com/2020/07/the-real-mud-on-golden-girls.html.

Today interview with the cast of *The Golden Girls*. Aired in 1987 on NBC.

Today interview with the cast of *The Golden Girls*. Aired in 1991 on NBC. Video, 3:36. https://www.youtube.com/watch?v=79Bal3lfnlw.

Towner, Betsy. "Betty White: My Life at the Zoo." *AARP Bulletin* (December 8, 2011). Accessed March 19, 2021. https://www.aarp.org/entertainment/books/info-12-2011/betty-white-life-at-the-zoo-author-speaks.html.

Trainer, David, dir. *Hot in Cleveland*. Season 2, episode 1, "Free Elka." Aired January 19, 2011, on TV Land.

—. *Hot in Cleveland*. Season 2, episode 2, "Bad Bromance." Aired January 26, 2011, on TV Land.

—. *Hot in Cleveland*. Season 2, episode 10, "Law & Elka." Aired March 23, 2011, on TV Land.

—. *Hot in Cleveland*. Season 3, episode 7, "Two Girls and a Rhino." Aired January 11, 2012, on TV Land.

—. *Hot in Cleveland*. Season 3, episode 19, "Bye George, I Think He's Got It!" Aired April 25, 2012, on TV Land.

U.S. Forest Service Press Office. "Forest Service Makes Actress Betty White Honorary Ranger." FS.USDA.gov. November 9, 2010. Accessed March 19, 2021. https://www.fs.usda.gov/news/releases/forest-service-makes-actress-betty-white-honorary-ranger.

Werts, Diane, interviewer. Interview with Mary Tyler Moore in New York, NY, Television Academy Foundation, October 23, 1997. Video, 29:09. https://interviews.televisionacademy.com/interviews/mary-tyler-moore.

White, Betty. *Betty & Friends: My Life at the Zoo*. New York: G. P. Putnam's Sons, 2011.

—, dir. *Betty White's Pet Set: The Complete Series*. 1971. MPI Home Video, 2021.

—. *Here We Go Again: My Life in Television*. New York: Scribner, 1995.

—. *If You Ask Me (And of Course You Won't)*. New York: G. P. Putnam's Sons, 2011.

—. *In Person*. New York: Doubleday, 1987.

—. Reddit AMA chat. April 28, 2014.

White, Betty and Tom Sullivan. *The Leading Lady: Dinah's Story*. New York: Bantam, 1992.

The Wilderness Society. "My Wilderness: Betty White Says Wilderness 'Is Where My Soul Lives.'" January 16, 2012. Video, 2:39. https://www.youtube.com/watch?v=9xF6AIKLMSY.

Winfrey, Oprah, interviewer. Betty White on *Oprah Winfrey's Where Are They Now?* Aired March 29, 2015, on Oprah Winfrey Network.

ABOUT THE AUTHOR

Paula Bernstein is the author of *Love is All Around: And Other Lessons We've Learned from The Mary Tyler Moore Show* and co-author of *Identical Strangers: A Memoir of Twins Separated and Reunited*. A former staff reporter at *Variety* and the *Hollywood Reporter*, her work has appeared in *Fortune*, *Fast Company*, the *New York Times*, and other publications. She lives with her family in Portland, Oregon. Visit her at paulabernstein.com.